I VOLUNTEERED FOR THIS

SOUTHWESTERN
LEGACY PRESS

ACKNOWLEDGMENTS:
Cover and Interior Design Services by Melinda Martin – Martin Publishing Services
REBOOT recovery veterans and first responders trauma healing can be found at REBOOTrecovery.com

ISBN: Paperback 978-1-7348118-3-4
Hardback 978-1-7348118-2-7
eBook 978-1-7348118-1-0

PUBLISHED BY:

SOUTHWESTERN
LEGACY PRESS

Southwestern Legacy Press, LLC
P.O. Box 1231
Gallatin, TN 37066
Email:swlegacypress@gmail.com

LIBRARY OF CONGRESS CONTROL NUMBER (LCCN) 2020920766
LIBRARY CATALOGING:
I Volunteered for This.
McCullough, Theresa Benner (Theresa Benner McCullough) – Author
156 pages 23cm × 15cm (9in. × 6 in.)

DESCRIPTION:
"I Volunteered for This" is the fascinating personal narrative of Theresa Benner McCullough's enlistment in the U.S. Army after college and subsequent deployment to Afghanistan with the 82nd Airborne brigade. One of only a handful of females at a remote base, Sarkari Karez, she was sexually assaulted by a male soldier one night. Then she had to deal with the invasive criminal investigation and insensitive male-dominated command structure to bring the "perp" to justice. Written in a personal journal style, each entry gives insight into the daily life of a young female soldier living in a war-torn combat zone. This book provides hope and encouragement to any woman who has experienced sexual trauma and is suffering from Post-Traumatic Stress Disorder (PTSD).

I VOLUNTEERED FOR THIS

A Woman's Perspective *of* Serving In the U.S. Army

THERESA BENNER MCCULLOUGH

SOUTHWESTERN
LEGACY PRESS

U.S. ARMY

This book is dedicated to anyone whose story was not believed, who was afraid to speak up, or who continues to suffer from sexual trauma. Our stories are all different, but they are, essentially, the same.

—Theresa Benner McCullough, Author

CONTENTS

U.S. ARMY

PART I

Enlisting

WHEN I WAS A YOUNG GIRL, ELEMENTARY SCHOOL STIRRED A DESIRE within me to be a teacher. That desire never diminished. As I grew older, I knew that teaching was what I had been made to do. I have an innate love for children and was sure my future would hold at least four of my own. Teaching wasn't just something I wanted to do; it was truly who I knew myself to be. When I was accepted into the elementary education program at Western Illinois University in Macomb, Illinois, I was ecstatic. With great expectations, I took this gigantic step on my journey toward my dream job. The first few education classes, however, stopped me on that path. As I learned about the mechanics of classroom teaching, I decided I didn't want to be a teacher after all. I found myself enrolled as a freshman in college with no idea of how to choose a new major. I had never considered another career, and since I saw myself as a teacher, I now felt lost.

After a great deal of contemplation, I switched my major to psy-

1

chology. I was intrigued by how the mind worked and learning more about that fascinated me. Supporting people dealing with mental health issues would definitely satisfy my inner desire to help others. There was no clearly defined image of where this degree would ultimately take me. So, I took a big leap of faith to find out. By the end of that first year, I also knew I wanted to live in a larger city, so I transferred to Illinois State University my sophomore year, and earnestly began working on my psychology degree. I submerged myself in my studies, and before I knew it, graduation was just a few months away, and I needed to plan my next step. I was torn between pursuing a master's degree or finding a job related to psychology. A master's program would mean an increase in my already high student loan debt. That was not a financially appealing outcome. Finding a job with only a bachelor's degree in psychology also would produce only minimal income. So, this was not a particularly appealing route for me.

Illinois State University had an ROTC program that prompted me to gather more information about enlisting in the military. I considered each of the five branches of services to figure out which would be the best fit for me. The Navy and Coast Guard were easy to eliminate since I am prone to seasickness. I agree with Mark Twain, "Seasickness: at first you are so sick you are afraid you will die, and then you are so sick you are afraid you won't die." So I couldn't envision doing my job while feeling sick most of the time. My fear of heights kept me from even considering the Air Force. The Marines just seemed way too intense to me. The remaining service was the U.S. Army.

Nutrition was another of my interests, and I began looking into pursuing a career in dietetics. I was encouraged when I learned the Army had a dietetic position offering the ability to pay back college loans or receive money for future schooling. I got more information online and then decided to meet with an Army recruiter in my hometown. Walking into the office displaying Army Strong posters featuring predominately male soldiers was very intimidating. As a 5'10", 125-pound female with absolutely no upper body strength, I certainly didn't relate to their images. My questions regarding the various jobs and training that the Army could provide were answered. However, I left the recruiting office feeling even more conflicted about the right path to take after graduation.

I went back to school knowing every day was one step closer to graduation, with the clock ticking down to the time when I had to decide what to do next.

I needed a plan, and maybe the Army was the answer. I would be able to receive a steady paycheck, live on my own, and earn money that could provide that needed master's degree. There were many positive aspects to that choice; however, I wasn't sure how I would tell my friends and family. I honestly could not imagine what my mother's reaction to this news would be. Would any of them even take me seriously? Could I take myself seriously? My personality didn't exactly have the traits one may think of when describing a soldier. I am an introverted female with an overly nice personality, an inability to do a push-up, and a fear of killing spiders or any bug for that matter. I know I shouldn't care about what others think, but I did. I sat down with my parents first and told them I was planning on enlisting in the Army. My mother was speechless and wasn't in favor of my joining the service. She invited me to move back home after graduation while I looked for a job. My father was resolved to the fact that I was an adult and didn't need their signatures to enlist. He left the decision up to me.

A few weeks later, I went back to the recruiting station to complete a physical training (PT) test to see if I were able to meet the physical standards. It consists of two minutes of push-ups, two minutes of sit-ups, and a two-mile run. Based on my age and gender, I needed a minimum number to pass the test. The push-up test was first, and the standards for females in my age group required me to complete thirteen push-ups. However, after two minutes, I only managed to do nine! The standard for push-ups was a ninety-degree elbow bend, which was very challenging with my lack of upper body strength. After I failed the push-up component, I did sit-ups. With a partner holding my ankles during the exercise, I managed to do forty-five sit-ups, which was passing.

The two-mile run was next, and I felt the most confident about this part. During high school, my father encouraged me to run cross country or track, but at that point in my life, I despised running. Running laps or ladders in the gym generally were punishment during the time I was on the basketball team. When I went to college, however, I developed a love of running. I ran in my free time, not because someone forced me too, but because I wanted to run. The run for the PT test was in a nearby park, and I was the only female out of about eight people. I finished in second place, and the recruiter was impressed by my time.

The final component of the PT test was a weight evaluation based on an individual's height. The minimum and maximum weight requirements are on a scale similar to a body mass index (BMI) chart. After the run, we returned to the recruiting station and were weighed and taped if needed. Taping was used for soldiers who were considered overweight on the BMI scale. These soldiers would need to be measured around their neck, waist, and hips to compare to standards. At 5'10" and 125 pounds, I was considered underweight, so there was no need to tape me. We were given feedback on what we should do to improve our scores. I was instructed to build my upper body strength and gain weight. It was a relief that pull-ups weren't part of the PT test. I didn't think an assisted weight machine would be allowed during the test, and I couldn't do them on my own. I went back to school and focused on my final weeks of college. It was strange to realize that this chapter of my life was ending so soon. I needed to either apply for a civilian job or enlist in the U.S. Army.

After graduation, I moved out of my college apartment and back to my parents' home. Then I one day returned to the recruiter station to complete my ASVAB exam. That stands for the Armed Service Vocational Aptitude Battery. A certain score on the exam is required to enlist in the Army and receive a job assignment. It was a computer-generated test, and some sections were easier for me than others. I was clueless when it came to the weapons and vehicle maintenance sections. I knew I wouldn't be qualifying for those positions, but I was determined to be assigned as a nutrition care specialist or dietitian. I passed the ASVAB so, my next step was to go to the Military Entrance Processing Station or MEPS.

As I entered MEPS, I felt more intimidated to walk into a building than ever before. The limited number of women was obvious, and the soldiers just looked more intimidating in uniform. I felt like everyone was looking at me, thinking, *What is someone like you doing enlisting in the Army?* I nervously waited until I was called for a physical with the other females who were enlisting. We first were escorted into a room and asked to strip down to our bras and underwear. The room was ice cold with one small heater in the corner. I wanted to keep my clothes on because it was so cold and also because I was surrounded by twenty strangers. We were asked to form up in a single file line. Two female soldiers came in with a scale and a clipboard. We each stepped on the scale, and they wrote down our weight and height. After each of us went on the scale, we stood on opposite sides of the room. We walked across, and I felt like I was modeling in a fashion show. However, they were not grading our walk but were looking for marks on our bodies that may disqualify us from enlisting. I was very happy once we were able to put our clothes back on, and I could be warm again.

We were then brought to the office where we would be choosing our military occupational specialty (MOS), which is another term for a job title. I only had one job in mind, and that was a nutrition care specialist, a 68M. However, the employee on the computer informed me that there were no open slots available for a 68M. Frankly, ever since then, I've wondered if that was a white lie, so I would have to choose a position that needed to be filled. He asked me if I had a second choice. I hadn't even thought about what my Plan B would be. He mentioned I could return later to see if there were any openings for the 68M position. I knew I didn't have time to wait for the position to open. The three available MOS's I could choose were a foodservice specialist, office worker, or supply clerk. Foodservice specialist sounded so fancy even though I was told it was a cook. The employee told me the foodservice specialist and nutrition care specialist attended the same advanced individual training (AIT). It is training that follows basic training and is specific to your MOS.

He also told me another white lie. He said I could switch my job once I was assigned to my unit. I believed him but would later find out that was not true. I decided to choose to be a 92G, foodservice specialist. I was then told that my basic training would be at Fort Sill, Oklahoma. I kept telling myself that it could always be worse. However, going to Oklahoma in the middle of August sounded awful to me.

After filling out more paperwork than you can imagine, I enlisted in the Army. However, it wasn't official until I was sworn in. The swearing-in ceremony occurred every hour, so I waited in the lobby, along with many other enlistees. As I was called into the room, we were instructed to stand arm's length away from the person next to us. We stood in silence until a sergeant walked to the front of the room. We all raised our right hand and swore we would defend the Constitution of the United States.

The common phrase "out of body experience" took on meaning for me that day. I felt like I was standing outside of the room, looking into a window watching myself become the property of the government. It was so intense to be doing this; I had to step outside the experience to grasp what was happening. The whole time the swearing-in ceremony was going on, I wondered if this was the right choice. I knew that I could deploy to a combat zone at any moment and risk my life. And for what? In order to pursue a career goal, receive a paycheck, or maybe just to be able to live on my own. In my effort to secure my future, I had entered into the most uncertain path imaginable. Uncertainty of what was to come was the most nerve-wracking part of what I was about to do. I had to not only trust my decision to take this step; I had to be willing to trust it for the next three years and twenty-three weeks. On August 8, 2011, I left my civilian life behind and became a soldier in the U. S. Army.

U.S. ARMY

PART II

Basic Training

AUGUST 8, 2011

SAY GOODBYE

TODAY WAS THE LAST DAY AT HOME WITH MY FAMILY BEFORE I LEFT for boot camp. I had more butterflies in my stomach than the day my parents dropped me off at college. I drove to the recruiter station in the morning to sign my official contract. Then I spent the day saying goodbye to friends, eating Giordano's pizza, and a carrot cupcake. I figured that would not be on the menu in the cafeteria at basic training. My mother, father, and sister dropped me off at the hotel where I would be spending the night. It was a sad experience to say goodbye to my family. I tried not to cry, but as soon as my mother hugged me, I lost it. Before I entered the hotel, I tried to regain my composure, then went to my assigned room.

I had a roommate that was also entering the service. She was eighteen years old and had just graduated from high school. I figured since I was twenty-two years old, I may be among the older recruits in my class. It has been impossible to sleep with thoughts racing through my head about the days to come. My roommate's loud snoring has been another reason for my sleeplessness.

AUGUST 9, 2011

FT. SILL

Today we had breakfast with the other recruits. It was very quiet in the lobby as everyone ate and prepared to board a bus. It drove us to the airport, and we were headed for Oklahoma. We were placed into groups of four and were instructed to stay together until we landed. A school bus picked us up at the airport, and we were driven to Fort Sill. I had no idea what to expect. Would it be like the movies or a television show, the drill sergeants yelling while the recruits look terrified? When the school bus pulled up, I saw a drill sergeant standing at attention. He looked sharp in his uniform and didn't even crack a smile or move.

Once the bus stopped, he stepped inside and said, "Welcome to Fort Sill. We will now begin inprocessing you. First, we will have a briefing in the building directly behind you. Once you get inside, file in and take a seat, starting in the front of the room to the back of the room. Do not pick up anything on the table and keep your mouths shut. Any questions?" No one said a word. Even if someone had a question, we were too afraid to ask.

As we stepped off the bus, it didn't take long to realize that Fort Sill was hot, humid, and more of a desert than I was used to. Once we were all seated, we were provided lunch. It was called a Jimmy Dean™, which reminded me of a child's lunchable. It consisted of a juice box, chips, applesauce, canned tuna, and a few cookies. As soon as the meals were passed around, we had ten minutes to eat it. The briefing started; we filled out paperwork, then we grabbed our bags to started the inprocessing.

In the first room, we were issued uniforms, shirts, socks, boots, hats, PT uniforms, underwear, and sports bras. In the next room, we were issued a pillow, sheets, blankets, towels, and washcloths. In the final room, we were issued a backpack, duffle bags, knee pads, elbow pads, vests, magazine holders, and a helmet. By the time we had finished gathering our equipment, it was nearly dark. The women were grouped together and were led to our barracks room. About half the room was occupied with females in various days of inprocessing. There were about twenty bunk beds in the main room, and we were instructed to pick the first available one. Today has been a long day, and I realize that from now on, every day will be long.

AUGUST 10, 2011

EARLY WAKE-UP

FOR THE FIRST TIME IN MY LIFE, I WAS AWAKENED AT 0400 HOURS ON purpose. It was a good thing I considered myself a morning person, but I could easily tell those who were not. We lined up outside in platoons based on what day of inprocessing we were in. My platoon was the furthest on the right and was considered the newbies. We were placed in a formation and prepared to march to the chow hall for breakfast.

While we were marching, the sergeant in charge of us started to call cadence. It was the first time besides the movies that I had heard a cadence. "Down by the river…" and we were marching along. It was a slow-moving line in the chow hall since it was the only one available. As we stood outside in line, we were instructed to remain silent and look forward. The sergeants walked around and talked to a few of the recruits.

"What is your name, and where are you from?" The sergeant said to me.

"My name is Specialist Benner, and I am from Chicago," I said.

"But you're white; you can't be from Chicago," the sergeant said while looking baffled.

"Actually, I am from the Chicago suburbs; I typically say Chicago because if someone is not from Illinois, they likely do not know where Wheaton is," I said.

"Oh, that makes more sense that you are from the suburbs," the sergeant added.

He was wrong to think that no white people live in Chicago. I kept my mouth shut after that, knowing it was probably frowned upon to argue with a sergeant.

As I entered the chow hall, I grabbed a tray, oatmeal, scrambled eggs, a banana, and toast with peanut butter and found a seat. We had about seven minutes to eat, which was something I needed to get used to. The hot oatmeal ended up burning my mouth as I tried to finish it quickly. We put our trays away and were instructed to fall back into formation. Then we marched to the Post Exchange (PX) store to buy toiletries and miscellaneous items. The options for running shoes were limited with two Asics™ brand shoes to choose from.

The building next to the PX was an ID photo station. In the Oklahoma heat, everyone was sweating, especially people coming from colder climates. I looked like a hot mess in my ID picture that I would have for the next three years. It was already lunchtime by the time we were finished with the pictures, and then we marched over to the chow hall.

In the afternoon, we had classes about marching and formation etiquette. Many people had gone to Reserve Officer Training Corps (ROTC) training, so it seemed to come more naturally for them. On the other hand, I was introduced to a brand-new world of information. It was dinner time, and we gathered into another formation and off we went to the chow hall. Following dinner, we had the evening off to shower, call our friends and family, and get some much-needed sleep.

The shower situation was unlike anything I had seen in high school or the universities I attended. It was a communal shower with about twelve shower heads mounted on the wall, reminding me of showers that are shown in prison movies. I knew the long hot showers that I found relaxing probably wouldn't be available in basic training. A cold shower surrounded by strangers was the new normal, at least for the inprocessing stage. I called my parents and got my clothes ready

15

for tomorrow. Before, I thought I might be a light sleeper, but after sleeping in a room with forty women, I now knew I was. I may be pushing my luck, but I am going to buy earbuds and a sleeping mask at the PX.

AUGUST 11, 2011

MEDICAL CHECKUP

WAKING UP BEFORE THE SUN BEGINS TO SHINE SEEMS NORMAL. After breakfast, we went to the clinic. In the waiting room, we were briefed about the vaccinations we would be receiving. Luckily for me, most of my shots were up to date from yearly physicals. I only had to receive four inoculations, but many people nearly doubled that number of shots. It was like an assembly line: we gave them our file, they wiped down our arm, gave us the shot, and we moved to the next vaccination. After I received my first shot, I saw a woman enlistee passed out in the waiting room. I hoped she only had to get one shot even though that probably wasn't the case. I left the clinic and honestly didn't know what vaccinations I received. After lunch, we went to the dental clinic. Since I was older than many of the others, my wisdom teeth had already been removed while I was in college. My dental visit was short since they didn't have to worry about my wisdom teeth. I also didn't have any cavities, so it turned out to be a pain-free visit.

Following our dental appointments, we had another briefing that discussed our finances. More specifically, it described how to read our leave and earning statement (LES), which was our paycheck. While in class, there were a few people who dozed off. However, I quickly learned that sleeping was not tolerated during classes. In the university setting, many of my professors didn't acknowledge when someone was sleeping. They simply continued the lesson and knew it was our responsibility to stay awake. But in the U.S. Army, you were called out and told to stand in the back of the room. I was already sleepy before the briefing, and the boring lesson about LES was not helping that. The sergeant mentioned that drinking water from our canteen would help keep us awake. At first, I was skeptical, but by the end of the class, my canteen was empty. I never considered myself much of a coffee drinker, but I never wanted a cup more than during the briefing. I completed the meeting without being called out, which I considered a win in my book. During dinner tonight, the only thing I thought about was my twin mattress with the green felt blanket and lumpy pillow.

AUGUST 12, 2011

BASIC BEGINS

TODAY WAS MY LAST EARLY MORNING WAKE UP FOR INPROCESSING. The sergeants were trying to scare us all week about what we should expect from our drill sergeants. I pictured the drill sergeants screaming and making recruits do push-ups. This was not an ideal situation for me since push-ups were not one of my strengths. After breakfast, we went back to our rooms and packed our bags. We were instructed to go to the bleachers and wait for the buses to arrive. We lined up alphabetically, and about thirty people created a platoon. Each platoon was given a different color basketball jersey. Red, yellow, green, and blue jerseys were handed out to everyone. Sitting on the bleachers wearing a red jersey, I could not stop fidgeting. Many of my close friends I just had made were in my platoon, which would help make it through basic training.

The buses pulled up near the bleachers, and four drill sergeants got off and walked towards the bleachers. I could hear the drill sergeants screaming at all of us to grab our bags and get on the buses. All that was going through my mind was, *What did I get myself into?* That only lasted about a second before I had to get on the bus or end up on the ground doing push-ups. Everyone ran as fast as they could to the bus, but it was difficult with the extra weight from our bags. The drill sergeants were constantly yelling at us, and I knew it was simply an intimidation technique. But even knowing this, I still was terrified of them. I threw my bag into the storage compartment under the bus and ran as fast as I could to find a seat inside. I started to daydream about my life as a civilian with my friends and family until the screams got too loud to ignore. This environment would be my reality for the next two months. My only option to get through it would be to have faith in myself and not let them break me. I knew it was a mind game, and I didn't even need my psychology degree to understand that.

Everyone was sitting quietly, and if there were crickets on the bus, you probably could have heard them chirping. It was a ten-minute drive, and then I looked out the window at my home away from home. I would miss the green grass, rain, and lower humidity back in Wheaton. We arrived at the barracks, and the yelling began again. This time we were instructed to get off the bus from the rear to the front. I could see the other four drill sergeants waiting outside, and to say they look frightening was just an understatement. It was complete chaos and something that seemed out of a movie or television show. We grabbed our bags and ran towards the barracks to file into a formation. At the same time, drill sergeants were yelling at the slower recruits. My heart was pounding as I stood in formation with my platoon.

The first sergeant of our company spoke a few words before the drill sergeants took over. Drill Sergeant Walton and Drill Sergeant Burns were assigned to my platoon. Drill Sergeant Walton looked like he could easily kill me, and it would be done quickly. On the other hand, Drill Sergeant Burns was more difficult to read. Drill Sergeant Walton began to read off our names from a clipboard, and that is the moment in my military life when my first name was nonexistent. "Brenner" was announced, and I knew better than to correct him and just said, "Here, Drill Sergeant."

It was time for the females and males to separate into our living quarters. I grabbed my bags and ran upstairs with the other women. As I entered the room, I stepped on a symbol painted on the floor. I could hear the female drill sergeant start to yell, and I was praying that it wasn't at me. However, it wasn't my lucky day. I learned that stepping on the symbol was strictly forbidden. "Leaning rest position move," was all she said, and I had no idea what that even meant. I assumed it was the push-up position, so, in other words, an exercise plank. That is the moment I met my battle buddy. Alphabetically, by name, she was put in the leaning rest position next to me. I hadn't said one word to her, and I was already getting her in trouble. While everyone else was finding their lockers and bed, I was doing a plank. After two minutes, which seemed like forever, we were told to stand up. After that, I avoided stepping on the symbol. The other females seemed to appreciate learning from my mistake too.

AUGUST 13, 2011

RADIO SILENCE

THE MORNING WAKE-UP WAS ANYTHING BUT PLEASANT. THE FEMALE drill sergeants came into our room and used a megaphone to wake us. It didn't take long to realize that beauty sleep wasn't going to be happening in basic training. We were told we had ten minutes to get dressed in our PT uniform and make our beds. It was absolute chaos as sixty females used the bathroom, better known as a latrine in the Army, to get ready. With six sinks and eight stalls, I was going to have to learn patience. We raced downstairs and went into formation with our platoon. The drill sergeants came out of the office and told us we had better be ready for our first PT test the following week. They warned us if we failed, it would be an automatic counseling statement. However, I learned later that counseling was nothing more than a slap on the wrist. We finished a morning run, and showering was the next on the schedule.

The showers had more privacy with individual stalls even though they were open. With only eight stalls, it was going to be quite challenging for sixty females to take showers in time for breakfast. We were told to wrap ourselves in our towel and stand in line. The female drill sergeant gave us each two minutes, which was the maximum amount of time for showering. That morning I learned that shaving my legs was not happening for a few months. We marched to the chow hall and silently waited in line. I had a feeling the limited amount of time at meals was going to be permanent. I opted to skip the oatmeal since burning my mouth did not seem like a great way to start my morning. We were seated, and I was relieved we weren't allowed to talk. I needed every minute to eat as much as I could before time was up. I had taken for granted being able to enjoy eating during meals. Once outside the chow hall, we took roll call and went back to the company.

We were instructed to grab our cell phones and go to the mail-room. Drill Sergeant Walton told us that we would have two minutes to call our parents. Then he said our phones would be taken away. Everyone went from pure happiness to almost disbelief. Someone asked if they could have more time if they couldn't reach anyone. "No, just leave a message," he stated.

As I heard the phone ring, I prayed that my dad would pick up the phone. It's how I imagine feeling on the show *Who Wants to Be a Millionaire* when they use the phone-a-friend lifeline. If the person doesn't pick up, you are SOL (shit out of luck). I was so thankful that my dad picked up, and it was great to hear his voice. I tried to be quick and told him I made it and that our phones would soon be taken away. He could hear the trembling in my voice. His last words to me were to stay strong and that he loved me. I could hear the megaphone as Drill Sergeant Walton told us to hang up.

As I looked around the room, I saw many tears but considered myself lucky since I was able to talk to my dad. The drill sergeant took away our cell phones, and everyone started to cry. We all said goodbye to texting, calling, and social media today, and tonight seems lonelier.

AUGUST 20, 2011

TREAD WALL TOWER

I'M ACCUSTOMED TO MY ROUTINE OF GETTING UP EARLY, PT, AND breakfast. However, this morning we were the last platoon to leave the chow hall, and Drill Sergeant Walton was not happy about it. We formed up and went to the tread wall tower. One of my greatest fears is heights, and hearing the word tower didn't make me think it was on the ground. Once we arrived, Drill Sergeant Walton had reached his limit of patience. It was unlike anything I had seen in real life before. At that moment, I thought about the drill sergeants from military-based movies. Within a few seconds of yelling at our platoon, he had us in the leaning rest position in the sand. He had us do push-ups, and I could feel myself start to tear up. As I looked around, there were not only sweat and dirt on faces, but tears. He told us we didn't deserve to be in basic training, and we were disappointments who would never become soldiers. It was the first time I thought to myself, *Why did I sign up for this hell?* I missed my family so much, and hearing the drill sergeants doubts only led me to start doubting myself.

After we wiped away our tears, I looked up at the tower that we were required to climb. We were put into harnesses, and I knew I was not getting out of doing this. We walked to the ladder on the backside of the wall. Next, it was my turn, and I just kept thinking, *Don't look down*. I tried to distract myself, but with each step of the ladder, it was harder to convince myself I was still on the ground. I made it to the top and crawled to a drill sergeant who attached a rope to my harness. I immediately regretted looking down, and I felt my heart fall to my stomach. A drill sergeant said, "Go," and I hesitated for a second. She said that I had to go, so I placed my feet on the wall and slowly walked down. I prayed there wouldn't be any mishap with the rope until my feet reached the ground. I smiled as it was over; I didn't think in a million years that I could face my fears. At that moment, I knew my drill sergeant had been wrong. I am going to become a soldier!

AUGUST 25, 2011

PT TEST

THE MORNING PT TEST IS FINALLY HERE. ALL WEEK DRILL SERGEANT Walton had been warning us that if we do not pass, then we would be counseled. All the females were nervous to say the least, because no one was speaking to one another. We were put in single file lines behind a drill sergeant who would grade us. I was hoping for an easy grader, but since they were drill sergeants, luck was probably not going to be in my favor. The first event was the push-up, and for my age group, I needed at least seventeen. I got in the plank position and waited until the drill sergeant said to begin and started to push. The first few push-ups were quite easy, but then I got to ten, and I could barely keep myself up. I only had thirty seconds left and seven push-ups to go, but my body was not strong enough. When I heard that the two minutes were up, I knew I had only done twelve push-ups and failed. At that moment, I thought that maybe I just wasn't cut out to be a soldier. All I wanted to do was go home. However, I still had the sit-ups and a two-mile run component for the test to be complete.

For the sit-up test, I needed fifty in the two-minute time frame. I tried to give it my best effort even though I knew to fail one event was ultimately failing everything. Once I went past fifty sit-ups, I knew I had passed. The two-mile run was the test I was least worried about. Unlike the other basic trainees in my platoon, I loved running. They all thought I was a little odd because they just saw running as punishment. I ended up beating most of the males, and the ones with an ego were pretty upset about it.

Later today about fifteen people from my platoon, including myself, were called to Drill Sergeant Walton's office. It reminded me of being sent to the principal's office, and my heart was pounding.

Drill Sergeant Walton looked even more disappointed than the day at the tread wall tower. I received my first counseling statement due to a PT failure. The corrective action was to pass the next one or else risk being recycled. Recycling means I will be transferred to another company that was in an earlier part of the training. I honestly don't think I can go through basic training longer than is required. I have a pact with another female who had failed the push-up test to do at least ten push-ups every hour until our next PT test.

SEPTEMBER 2, 2011

RIFLE RANGE

A S WE WOKE TO THE POURING RAIN, THE THOUGHT OF GOING TO THE weapons firing range was not very appealing to me. However, having an opinion about anything went out the window once I was sworn into the service. I went to the shooting range once with my father and still remember the bruises I had from the rifle's recoil. We received our M-4 from the armory and three empty magazines. The march to the range seemed much longer with the extra weight we were carrying.

Once we arrived, we were given some basic instructions to follow while on the firing line. What I took away from it was not to point the weapon anywhere except downrange. The fact that they told us that means someone or more likely more than one person violated that rule. It made me feel slightly better that we were wearing our vest. Then I thought someone could easily shoot a different part of my body, and that slightly better feeling immediately went away.

At the range, we had to shoot and knock down at least twenty-three out of forty pop-up targets to pass. If we were not successful, we would have to keep shooting until we received a score of twenty-three. For some, it was a piece of cake, while others were out at the range for what seemed like forever. It was my turn, and I just prayed that no one would shoot me. The closer targets started dropping once I shot them, which made me feel good, but then the 400-meter targets popped up. With the rain and fog, the 400-meters never seemed to fall. I already had a bad feeling as I headed to the tower to hear how I did.

"Brenner, fifteen, try again," the drill sergeant said.

I tried to think positively and reminded myself that for my second time shooting, fifteen wasn't bad. On the other hand, it wasn't good enough to pass basic training. As I walked to shoot again, I prayed that I would get at least twenty-three.

"Brenner, nineteen, try again," the drill sergeant said.

Well third time's the charm, right? At least, so they say. My third time on the range and my hands were numb due to the cold rain. As soon as the targets started popping up, I thought about the people who had doubted my ability to become a soldier. Even some of my fellow battle buddies didn't think I was physically tough enough to be a solider. During those two minutes, I completely zoned out and simply focused on my M-4 and the targets. As I walked to the tower, I felt confident that I had passed.

"Brenner, twenty-five, good job, finally," the sergeant said with sarcasm.

I'm impressed with my score. Maybe I should give myself more credit for making it this far. There were always going to be people who would doubt me; I'm definitely going to start believing in myself!

SEPTEMBER 4, 2011

SUNDAY CHURCH

SUNDAY IS MY FAVORITE DAY IN BASIC TRAINING. IT BEGINS WITH church, and I can choose from a variety of services to attend. If you chose not to go to church, then you were stuck at the barracks on cleaning detail.

Most people seemed to go even if they weren't religious. My battle buddy and I took a bus to the Catholic Church. I had never seen a church so packed, but it wasn't surprising since barracks cleaning was the only alternative. After the service, there was an optional focus group that we could attend. We weren't exactly sure we wanted to go, but once we heard there would be snacks, we were all in. It was a very peaceful environment that I wasn't accustomed to. I was ready for the person in charge of the focus group to make us do push-ups. However, that was not the case. We talked about life issues and had lots of cookies and candy. Dessert is never an option for us in the cafeteria, so today was a treat.

SEPTEMBER 6, 2011

NOT GLAMPING

THE WALK TO THE TRAINING FIELD STARTED BRIGHT AND EARLY, OF course. We packed our bags for two nights of sleeping in tents. This wasn't going to be "glamping." We ate a quick breakfast before we strapped our rucksack to our back and started marching. As we marched to the field site, we practiced walking in tactical formation. We had to pretend as if enemies were in the area we were marching by. It was very difficult for me to imagine since we were in Oklahoma. However, I played along with the drills and acted as if enemies were hiding in the field. Talking was not allowed while we were marching in tactical formation. It made sense, but the only distraction I had was the lack of scenery at Fort Sill. Most of the time, daydreaming did the trick. I imagined what I would be doing with my life instead of marching with thirty pounds strapped to my back.

When we finally arrived at the campsite, all I wanted to do was sleep, but that was out of the question. We dropped off our gear in the tent and headed out for some training. We practiced entering and clearing a room. We lined up in groups of four and each person who entered looked at a different area within the room. If you think about any police or military movies where they enter a house looking for bad guys, that was what we did.

The next type of training was learning how to properly search a car that enters a base. We learned how to look for improvised explosive devices or IEDs on vehicles. My drill sergeant mentioned that food-service specialists who didn't cook on deployment ended up searching vehicles. I pretended like I already knew that, but deep down, I was terrified that I would be blown up by an IED while deployed. I normally am very detailed in my letters to my parents, but I figured it will be better if I don't tell them about this.

After we ate chow, we headed back to our tents. A few females asked to turn on the lights, but flashlights were the only way to see. Before we went to bed, we used our flashlight to check our battle buddies for ticks. Of all the things I thought we might be doing today, I never imagined I would be doing that.

SEPTEMBER 7, 2011

MRE TRADES

AFTER SLEEPING ON THESE COTS IN THE FIELD, EVERYONE IS READY to go back to the company. We still have a full day of training before we marched back.

After breakfast, we headed back out to the field to practice tactical drills. After a few hours, we had meals ready to eat (MREs) for lunch. MREs are packaged meals commonly used in the field that include a variety of entrees, drinks, crackers, bread, and dessert. The MREs include a burner, which allows the food to be heated with water. Only a few of the meals had candy such as M&Ms and Skittles, so a lot of exchanging occurred. It was like we were back in the elementary school cafeteria trading parts of our lunches. Everyone loved to trade with me since I enjoyed the dried cranberries as opposed to the candy.

After feeling like kids for a few minutes, we went inside to practice shooting on a virtual reality game. It was nice to be inside since the weather was getting hotter. The instructors were civilians and were much less intimidating than the drill sergeants. Afterward, we marched back to the tents and checked each other for ticks again before going to bed.

SEPTEMBER 8, 2011

RUCK OUT

W E PREPARED TO MARCH BACK TO THE COMPANY BUT HAD TO WAIT for another unit to leave before us. As we saw them march by, some of their bags looked like they were filled with pillows, which clearly didn't weigh thirty pounds. It seemed like a smart idea, but our drill sergeants checked our rucksacks before we left. After returning to the company, it was a great feeling to know that I marched back without cheating. I dropped my rucksack, and the weight was instantly lifted from my shoulders. We stood in formation to take accountability and then went upstairs to put our gear in our lockers. However, we still had a full day of training ahead of us. We sat in the company and listened to the commander talk about combatives. He informed us that we would be learning and practicing the basics tomorrow. As a non-confrontational individual, the fighting doesn't interest me at all, but I know I have to play along and pretend like I'm interested.

SEPTEMBER 9, 2011

COMBATIVES

THE FIRST THING ON MY MIND WHEN I WOKE UP TODAY WAS THAT WE are starting combatives. I wish I could fast forward time. We marched to the field that was across the street. It doesn't matter the distance we traveled as a platoon, and we always marched. We sat and listened to the drill sergeants demonstrate basic techniques and combative moves. After watching our instructors, it was time to practice. We split up in two circles, and the person on the inside faced the outside individual. The first person I was paired with was a male who was much larger than me. Our drill sergeant gave us the signal to begin even though most of us didn't have a clue what we were doing. The male literally knocked me down and then sat on me. It was an unfair advantage from the start. Luckily, we moved on to the next partner quickly.

I was paired with a female who was about my height but clearly had more upper body strength. I gave it my best effort but was still defeated. I am normally a competitive person, but I knew from the beginning that during combatives, I would likely lose. We only have a few days of training until we have a tournament. I have a feeling I won't be making it very far in the tournament, and that's okay with me.

SEPTEMBER 12, 2011

PT TEST STRESS

I WOKE UP WITH KNOTS IN MY STOMACH. THE FEMALE BAY WAS QUIETER than I could remember. Everyone was focused since today was the last PT test. If I fail, I will be recycled into a different company. With all the good friends I have made thus far, I don't want to leave, so failing is not an option. I went downstairs with the other females and formed up for roll call. After figuring out that no one had run away overnight, we lined up behind a drill sergeant for the PT test. The first event was push-ups, which I had failed last time. All I needed was seventeen push-ups in the two-minute time frame.

"Ready? Begin," the drill sergeant stated.

I knew I had to pace myself so I wouldn't tire myself out too quickly.

"One-minute remaining" was announced.

I counted to myself seventeen push-ups, but then I heard,

"Twelve, twelve, twelve, twelve," the drill sergeant repeated.

The push-up criteria were based on having your elbow form a 90-degree angle. If the drill sergeant didn't feel that you met the criteria, then it would not count. I tried to focus on lowering my body so that the last few push-ups would matter. When the two minutes were complete, I had done nineteen push-ups and passed the first component, but I knew it was too early to celebrate.

The sit-up event was next, and I was very nervous. I learned that day when I am nervous, I pee, which explains my multiple trips to the latrine. I laid down on the ground while a male held down my ankles. I never understood why we didn't just put our feet under a bar. The drill sergeant usually let me go to the back of the line instead of holding someone's ankle. An individual with limited upper body strength will most likely hinder rather than help their performance. I had to get a minimum of fifty sit-ups, which may seem easy. However, I came to understand sit-ups are not the same as crunches. If the grader was tough, then the form needed to be perfect.

I heard, "Ready? Begin." I gave it my best shot. As I started to do a few sit-ups, I realized how awkward it is for someone to hold your ankles. As you do a sit-up, you have to avoid hitting your heads together. Two minutes had come and gone, and I was happy to know that I had done sixty sit-ups.

The final event was the two-mile run, and I was excited to run my heart out. We had to put on jerseys so the drill sergeant would be able to distinguish us in the crowd of runners. Every group had a different saying that needed to be said as we crossed the mile mark and then again when we had finished the run. The drill sergeant in charge of my group wanted us to say, "I heart Hannah Montana," and many of the males were not too thrilled about that.

I had run a lot of races in my life, but I felt like I had much more on the line today. I completed the first lap in a great time and confessed my love for Hannah Montana. On the second lap, I just thought about getting to the finish. When I had confessed my love for Hannah Montana once more, I knew that it was over, and I had passed the PT test. I wanted to cry. I congratulated my battle buddies who had passed and tried to encourage the ones who didn't. They are going to be recycled to another company, but at least they will have another chance to finish basic training.

OCTOBER 7, 2011

FINAL RUCK MARCH

TODAY WE HAVE THE LAST REQUIREMENT FOR GRADUATION, OUR final ruck march. It all came down to a fifteen-kilometer march with fifty pounds in our rucksack. I put bandages on my heels and toes to prepare for the blisters I would get. We started the march at 0200 hours due to the heat. Like other marches, there was no talking, and this time only the moon and stars were visible. Basic training was a mind game from the beginning, and this march was more mentally challenging than physically. It was too easy to stop walking and give up, but I tried to think about why I was doing this. I was told before I joined that I wouldn't make it because I was a weak female. I knew I had to finish the ruck march for myself, my family, and the people who doubted me. I believe that everything happens for a reason, and I was meant to be here and to graduate basic training.

We took a quick water break at mile three, which made it harder to start walking again.

As we continued to march, I tried to think about anything but the pain in my feet and back. The rucksack was more uncomfortable than I had imagined. The screws holding the sack together kept poking me in the back. I could feel the bruises coming, but I knew that it would be over soon. When I was younger, I had a favorite quote that helped me overcome obstacles in my life:

> *"Pain is temporary. It may last a minute, or an hour, or a day, or a year, but eventually, it will subside, and something else will take its place. If I quit, however, it lasts forever."*

> —LANCE ARMSTRONG

I repeated this quote to myself as I marched those last few miles. I knew the pain I was feeling would soon be over. I could hear my drill sergeant scream that we were almost to the company. I was running on pure adrenalin as I marched the last block. The greatest feeling in the world was removing the rucksack from my back. We all stood tall and proud in formation, knowing that we had accomplished the final task of our training.

OCTOBER 20, 2011

PARENTS' DAY

Parents' Day has finally arrived, and I'm excited to see my family. My mother and father must really love me if they flew all the way to Fort Sill, Oklahoma. We formed up in our platoons while our drill sergeants called some cadences. We were then released to visit with family. We had to be back at the company at 2000 hours that night, or else we would be punished. They warned us that if we were late, we would not be allowed to spend time with our families following graduation.

I hugged my parents until they told me to let go, but it didn't seem quite long enough. They were thrilled to see me and even more excited to show me the upgraded rental car they were driving. The rental company gave my parents a Mustang convertible, which made up for the fact that we would be exploring the town of Lawton, Oklahoma, near Fort Sill.

I had to stay in uniform all day, so I stuck out like a sore thumb. The first thing I wanted to do was get a pedicure and my eyebrows done. I felt bad for the nail technician since after rucking around Oklahoma, my feet were not pretty. It was wonderful to have some much-needed pampering and relaxation after training. We went to lunch, and I was excited to eat outside of the dining facility. I was craving barbecue, so we went to one of the few BBQ restaurants in town where I ordered pulled pork and sweet potato fries. Since I was used to having five minutes to eat, I scarfed down my meal. It took some time to realize that I wasn't being timed while I ate my meals that day. After lunch, we drove to a nearby bakery. I had been deprived of sugar since arriving at basic training. Luckily there was a bakery in town called the Cupcake Eatery. I ordered one of my favorite cupcakes, pumpkin spice, and reminded myself to savor every bite. After I got some sugar in me, we went to the Fort Sill History Museum. It was interesting to learn about the town even though I had no desire to return after basic training.

We explored the town some more before going to dinner. Since I had to be back at the company area at 2000 hours, I opted for a restaurant near the base, Texas Roadhouse™, because I enjoyed eating peanuts and throwing the shells on the floor. The entire time I felt like a drill sergeant was going to come up behind me and make me do push-ups for littering. We received the check, and I mentioned that I would love to wear make-up while in my uniform. We drove by Walgreens™, and then I knew we really needed to head back to the company. My father drove as I was freaking out in the backseat. Once we got near the base, he didn't know which entrance to take to get back to my company. I also had no idea how to get back there since today was my first time off base. I immediately called my battle buddy, who had a better sense of direction than I do, and she led us to the correct entrance. I had about five minutes to spare as I was dropped off at the company. I felt incredibly lucky as I stood in formation and saw we were missing a few people.

OCTOBER 21, 2011

GRADUATION DAY

WHEN I STARTED BASIC TRAINING, I NEVER IMAGINED I WOULD successfully complete the graduation requirements. I could barely do a push-up and had only gone to a shooting range once before arriving at basic. I was determined to prove to others and myself that I could finish the training. In the beginning, I lacked self-confidence, but now I recognized that I could do anything that I set my mind to.

It was a bit chaotic in the female room as we prepared for graduation. Females were putting on makeup and wearing earrings for the first time in months. We filed on to the bus and went to the Sheridan Theater, where the graduation was being held. In the auditorium, I tried to find my parents, but we were told to stare straight ahead as we walked down the aisle. As we sat down, everyone's parents were at the front, taking pictures. I saw my mom right away, but I knew I was being watched and couldn't speak or even smile.

The commander started by talking about the history of the company and specifically our class. The drill sergeants marched in and introduced themselves to the audience. I can still remember the day I met Drill Sergeant Walton and how I was utterly terrified of him. Now seeing him on the stage reminded me how I would not be graduating without his support. As I stood to walk across the stage and receive my diploma, it was another surreal moment in my life. I never doubted myself when I began classes at Western Illinois University, but I did once I began basic training. It was my time to cross the stage and shake Drill Sergeant Walton's hand. "Congrats, Benner," he said with a smirk.

He had called me Brenner from day one, and it meant so much to hear my actual name. His words will stay with me forever. Once we finished the ceremony, we were escorted back onto the bus. Our friends and family were instructed to meet us in the company area. We lined up in formation, and the drill sergeants wanted to punish us once more in front of our loved ones. My mom, of course, took pictures of my platoon doing push-ups. Luckily, he only made us complete ten push-ups. Little did our loved ones know that it was the least amount we ever had to do.

We had until about 1900 hours to spend with our family before we had to return to the company. I immediately wanted some ice cream, and you could say that I was on a sugar high afterward. My parents left for their flight around 1500 hours, so I spent time with one of my friends and her family. It was wonderful seeing my parents, and it was quite hard to say goodbye.

My friend and I went back to their hotel and relaxed by watching a movie. For dinner, we went to Olive Garden™ and enjoyed our last night out. We knew we would be leaving for the airport later tonight to start Advanced Individual Training. My friend's parents dropped us off at the company, and we waited for our taxi to the airport. I am flying to Fort Lee, Virginia, with the other foodservice specialists. I feel ready for the next adventure, but I am just as excited to be leaving Oklahoma.

U.S. ARMY

PART III

AIT Begins

OCTOBER 22, 2011

FT. LEE

I arrived at Fort Lee, Virginia, in the early morning with the other foodservice specialists. We were immediately bused to the base following the flight. The views from the bus were very vibrant with greens and flowers near the road. It was much more colorful than Fort Sill.

We were dropped off at our barracks as the other recruits were calling cadences. Four platoons were at different stages of training. Since we just started the training, we lined up behind the other three platoons. The commander of our company said a few words, and then we were dismissed. The females in my platoon rushed upstairs to find bunks and roommates to live with for the next couple of months. I ended up in a top bunk with five other roommates.

Once we knew our living arrangements, we received sheets, a blanket, and a pillow. I never thought making a bed was challenging until I was on the top bunk and attempting to fold hospital corners. We marched over to the dining facility, which was right across the street from the barracks. It was so nice having a few extra minutes to eat and to talk with other recruits at the table. I ended up eating as fast as I did in basic training, and I thought it probably would take some time to adjust. We were even able to walk back to the barracks following dinner, which felt like I was breaking the rules. It has been an exhausting, long day, and sleep is the perfect way to end it.

NOVEMBER 1, 2011

NO CONTRABAND

I AM ADJUSTING WELL TO LIFE IN FORT LEE. IT WAS NICE TO HAVE more freedom and perform fewer push-ups then during basic training. We marched to the PX and were able to buy a few items. However, once we went back into formation, our bags were searched. We were not allowed to have what they called contraband, which included candy, soda, and food of any kind. The other platoons had warned us that they searched the barracks every few weeks for contraband in our rooms. With that in mind, I purchased toiletry items and cough drops, which were the closest thing to candy. After everyone's bags were searched, we went back to the barracks.

Today we began our classes to learn skills to become foodservice specialists. Different parts of the classes must be passed before I can move on to the next class. First, we learn basic kitchen procedures, including safety and sanitation. The next parts will be cooking, baking, and batch cooking. With the weather getting cooler, it was nice that classes were held inside. I am not a fan of the cold. I grew up in Chicago, but that doesn't mean I like the cold.

NOVEMBER 15, 2011

NO SMOKING

IN HIGH SCHOOL AND COLLEGE, I EXPERIENCED DRAMA, BUT IT WAS nothing compared to the drama here at Fort Lee. Smoking was allowed in designated smoking areas behind the barracks. However, there are always rule breakers, and one female decided to smoke in the bathroom. The sergeants frequently checked our barracks, and the smell of cigarettes was easily detected by them.

Walking through the barracks, my platoon sergeant happened to notice the smell at 2300 hours when everyone was asleep. Without considering the time, she instructed all the females to get into formation outside. There was a frost outside, so I was hoping we wouldn't be standing in formation long. The sergeant walked outside, and before she even spoke, I sensed she was angry. We were told that a female smoked in the bathroom, and we weren't leaving the formation until someone came forward. She gave us a few moments to ourselves, which she hoped would give someone the courage to tell the truth, but no one said a word. We stood in formation for the next two hours, and I was even tempted to say something so that we could go inside.

Around 0100 hours the sergeant said this wasn't over, but we had to get at least a few hours of sleep before PT tomorrow. I am going to have a rough morning and probably a rough few days to come until someone admits they smoked inside.

NOVEMBER 16, 2011

ROOM SEARCHED

I WAS NOT SURPRISED THAT WE HAD A CONTRABAND INSPECTION THIS morning. We were instructed to stay downstairs while the sergeants went through every room. A few minutes later, they came downstairs with a garbage bag full of candy, cookies, and soda. At least this time, they knew who the contraband belonged to since it was stored in the ceiling tiles above a room. I was relieved it wasn't any of the females in my room since we would all be punished for it.

We were finally allowed to go upstairs once they finished searching the rooms. As I passed each room, I could see mattresses thrown on the floor and personal items from lockers on the ground. I noticed my mattress was on the ground, and I dreaded having to remake my bed with the perfectly squared hospital corners.

In the afternoon, we lined up in formation to receive our mail. If we received letters, the sergeant immediately gave it to the individual, but packages were a different story. It was usually fun to see the sergeants go through the care packages and find contraband. I told my mother about the rules regarding contraband. However, I specifically mentioned to her that if hidden well, they probably wouldn't find it. My favorite cookies are pink dipped madeleines from a bakery located near my grandmother. I knew one of two things would happen. Either they wouldn't find them or they would find them and throw them out. I felt it was worth the risk, and when I heard my name called, I stepped forward. He searched through my box quickly and didn't notice the contraband my mother had hidden. I knew it was best not to share since who knows who would snitch and rat me out. I hid the cookies in my locker and will have a couple each day while my roommates are out of the room. The cookies won't last long since it is impossible for me to have just one.

DECEMBER 3, 2011

WEEKEND PASS

IN AIT, WE HAVE MUCH MORE FREEDOM THAN BASIC TRAINING. WITH good behavior, we can leave the base for the weekend as a reward. A group of my friends decided to book a hotel room. We had to take a cab to get to the hotel since Uber™ and Lyft™ services weren't available. Once we checked into the hotel, we grabbed dinner at a local restaurant. Following dinner, we chose to spend time at an arcade. My favorite part of the weekend was sleeping on a comfortable mattress. Not having to make my bed or do hospital corners almost felt wrong.

We went back to the barracks and waited in the lounge for our sergeant, who had our assignments where we would be stationed next. I was quite nervous since we would be stationed at our new base for not just a few months, but years.

At the beginning of AIT, we had to create a wish list of bases. My top three were Fort Jackson in South Carolina, Hawaii, and Germany. I knew if I were stationed overseas, I would rarely see my family. Yet I also knew I would probably never have an opportunity like that again.

I received my orders for Fort Bragg. My first thought was that I had no idea where Fort Bragg was. The male soldier next to me told me it was in North Carolina. I was pleased once I knew my assignment because I was going to be close to extended family in South Carolina and still be able to travel back to Illinois. However, my emotions quickly changed once that same soldier said I was going to be in the 82nd Airborne Division. I made the connection and realized they would make me airborne. I tend to stay away from roller coasters, ferris wheels, and really anything moving above ground. The idea of jumping out of a perfectly good airplane was not appealing to me.

I called my family, and they were thrilled to hear I would be living in the United States for the next couple of years. I could hear my sister in the background saying she would love to jump out of airplanes for free. Both my brother and sister paid money to skydive, but I would rather pay money to stay on the ground.

DECEMBER 16, 2011

AIT GRADUATION

GRADUATION DAY IS HERE! I HAVE A LOT TO BE PROUD OF; NOT ONLY am I graduating, but I am the top student in the class. I knew this would be the last day I would see most of my friends. I have even been with a few since basic training, so it seems strange that our time together was over. My training at Fort Lee was cut a few weeks short so that we could graduate before Christmas. At the time, it seemed great, but we skipped the field training, which seems like a crucial part.

Nevertheless, we graduated with a quick ceremony in front of a few loved ones. We packed our bags, said our goodbyes, and I flew back to Chicago. I have really missed my family, and it will be wonderful to be back for the holidays and to experience a white Christmas.

When I arrived home, my best friends were there waiting to surprise me. I am shocked and feel so blessed to have amazing people in my life who would visit me the first second they had the chance.

DECEMBER 29, 2011

FT. BRAGG

I FLEW FROM CHICAGO, ILLINOIS, TO FAYETTEVILLE, NORTH Carolina. When I arrived in Fayetteville, I took a taxi to Fort Bragg. I was ready to be able to make my bed on my terms, among other things. Once I arrived, I immediately went to reception, where they had specific barracks for new recruits for inprocessing. I'll spend a week at reception, setting up my finances, attending a few seminars, and completing medical examinations. We are required to get everything done within the week's timeframe. If we don't, then a sergeant will take us to our appointments.

Once I complete the checklist, either by myself or with a sergeant, I will be able to move to my unit. I'm determined to finish my checklist in a few days, so I will be able to catch up on sleep and relaxation until time to move to my unit.

JANUARY 5, 2012

4TH BDE. DELTA TROOP

A MALE FOODSERVICE SPECIALIST AND I MOVED DOWN THE STREET TO the 82nd Airborne Division, 4th Brigade, Delta Troop. I was nervous about meeting my chain of command, and it helped to not be the only new soldier. We met our commander, first sergeant, and sergeant first class. The commander focuses on the troop operations, the first sergeant deals with soldiers, and our sergeant first class oversaw the cooks in the dining facility.

Within the troop, there were twelve foodservice specialists, and among those, only two women, including myself. Once we met most of our chain of command, we were shown to our barracks room. I didn't have a roommate at the time since there were still new recruits arriving in the unit. We went back to the unit for the final formation, and the first words out of my commander's mouth shook my world.

"In six weeks," he said, "we will be leaving for Afghanistan."

I knew when I signed up for the service there was a real possibility I could be deployed. I knew I had to tell my family once I returned to my barracks room. I had no idea how hard it would be, especially since my mother wasn't thrilled about my joining in the first place.

We talked for a few minutes before I told them I would be deploying. I could tell my parents were at a loss for words. Even at that time, I wasn't even sure where or how long we would be deployed. I talked to them for only a few minutes since I was quite emotional. I'm going to bed, hoping the commander's words were just a dream.

JANUARY 9, 2012

DEPLOYMENT ANNOUNCED

K NOWING THAT WE ARE DEPLOYING NEXT MONTH, WE ARE ALL AWARE we have a limited amount of time to cook before we leave. I was assigned to slicing carrots on the mandolin for a salad, which seemed easy. But then I noticed it was for a two hundred serving recipe.

As I was slicing carrots, I noticed a guy look at me from across the kitchen. I knew it was simply because I was a new female in a kitchen where we were the minority. He came up to me and talked to me for a few seconds until a sergeant told him to leave me alone.

After serving lunch, we fell into formation to discuss the upcoming deployment. We were given paperwork to complete, which included a will for deployment. It was very morbid to have to decide what I would be buried in, who would say my eulogy, and what songs would be playing. It was something no twenty-two-year-old wants to deal with. However, in war, there is death, and it is better to be prepared for the worst.

JANUARY 20, 2012

FIRST BOYFRIEND

I AM GETTING USED TO THE ROUTINE OF WORK AND PREPARING FOR deployment. It was nice to have a guy for a distraction, though. He was sweet and told me I was beautiful. I didn't know him very well, but I wanted to think about anything except the reality of deployment. He wanted me to be his girlfriend, and I said yes. He didn't know that he was my first boyfriend. I was vulnerable with him, and it was nice to have someone to talk to. He had deployed before, and it comforted me to hear that I was going to be okay.

We spent weekends together watching movies in the barracks and simply being together. It was hard not to think about the fact that we both would be leaving in about a month. I am trying just to enjoy the present as much as I can. I'm also trying not to focus too much on the upcoming deployment.

FEBRUARY 4, 2012

UNWANTED ADVANCE

M Y BOYFRIEND INVITED ME TO A SMALL GET TOGETHER HIS FRIEND was having off the post. He picked me up, and we drove to the PX and picked up some beer. Once we arrived at his friend's house, I was introduced to a few of his friends. The hosts made pasta and garlic bread, and I opted for wine instead of beer. We just hung out and talked while the men played video games.

Jell-O™ shots the hosts made earlier were passed around. They did not agree with my stomach, and I ended up vomiting in the bathroom. My boyfriend, who was the last person I wanted to see at that time, held my hair. How romantic that the first time we go out, he sees me looking like a hot mess. The later it got, I realized that we were staying the night. My boyfriend was in no shape to drive, and I just wanted to go to sleep anyways. The couple who were hosting went to their bedroom to sleep. I ended up crashing on one couch, and their friend was on another couch. My boyfriend got the short stick and ended up sleeping on the floor.

Everyone, including me, had been asleep for an hour or so when I felt someone touching me. His hand went down my pants, and my body froze. I thought it was my boyfriend, and I was not comfortable being intimate with someone else in the room. However, as soon as I heard his voice, I knew it was not my boyfriend. It was their friend who was sleeping on the couch next to me. He was completely wasted, and I also remembered that he was married.

"No, stop that," I whispered.

He was much stronger than me, and with his body on top of mine, I was unable to move.

"No! What about your wife?" I stated.

"She doesn't matter to me," he slurred.

"Please stop and just go back to sleep," I pleaded.

For some reason, he did that and stumbled back to the couch and fell asleep. However, I lay awake, staring at the ceiling. I remember the briefing we received at the unit about reporting sexual assault. Should I report him? I knew he was my boyfriend's friend, and I didn't want to hurt him either. How would his wife feel? Would my boyfriend even believe me? He had only known me for a few weeks while he had known his friend for years.

The next morning I decided not to say anything about the incident. His friend didn't say anything to me either. I never knew if it was because he was too drunk to remember or if he was simply embarrassed to tell his friend.

My boyfriend took me home, and I tried to forget about what happened. I knew I was leaving for deployment in a few weeks, and I was hoping I wouldn't have to see his friend again. I didn't know that I would have to work with him in the dining facility after our deployment.

U.S. ARMY

PART IV

This is Real Life

FEBRUARY 17, 2012

LAST HOME WEEKEND

THIS IS MY LAST WEEKEND BEFORE DEPLOYMENT, AND MY PARENTS and sister came to visit. I showed them around the base and my barracks room, which is packed and ready for the move. We stayed in a hotel room in Fayetteville, and it was nice to get away from the base, even if only for the weekend. We spent a day in Raleigh eating some southern cooking and exploring the capital.

When my family had to leave, all I could think about was that I might never see them again. I wanted so desperately for them to take me back to Wheaton so I could be a civilian again. I don't think I am mentally ready for war. I am very sure I'm not ready to die yet. I have so much left I want to do in my life, but I also know that no one forced me to sign up for the U.S. Army. Deployment has always been a very real possibility, and I have to be brave for myself and my family and to return home safe and sound.

FEBRUARY 19, 2012

READY TO DEPLOY

IN A FEW DAYS, I WILL BE LEAVING FOR AN EIGHT-MONTH DEPLOYMENT to Kandahar, Afghanistan. It still seems strange that my deployment is right around the corner. I have only vague ideas of what it will be like from military-based movies and television shows I have seen. I feel anxious, nervous, and excited, but the scariest thing is not knowing what to expect. The one thing I know for certain is my friends and family will always be there for me. It is tremendously helpful to have so many people thinking of me and wishing me well. I hope this deployment will go by fast. I can only pray that everyone makes it back home safe and sound.

FEBRUARY 24, 2012

24 HR. WORLD CROSSING

Fort Bragg to Shannon, Ireland
Shannon, Ireland to Bishkek, Kyrgyzstan

I HAD FINALLY MADE IT TO KYRGYZSTAN AFTER A LONG DAY OF traveling. Ireland was always on my bucket list to see, but we were not allowed to go sightseeing during our layover. Once we arrived at the Manas International Airport, we traveled to the Transit Center at Manas. It was an Air Force Base where in and out processing took place when you arrive and depart Afghanistan. I was not expecting the minus six-degree weather or snow but was told to enjoy it before we left for the warmer weather in Afghanistan.

We were assigned to tents and given sheets and a pillow. The base had a chapel, gym, twenty-four-hour cafeteria, coffeehouse, PX, library, and internet cafe. It was unexpected even to have internet available in our tents. The rest of the day was ours to sleep, shower, eat, and recover from the jet lag. We have been told tomorrow we will be participating in Humvee rollover training. I completed it before we deployed and still had the bruises to prove it.

We won't be in Kyrgyzstan long, and the tentative plan is to leave Sunday morning for Afghanistan. I am trying to be optimistic about the situation, and thinking about warmer weather caused me to smile.

FEBRUARY 26, 2012

HURRY UP AND WAIT

I QUICKLY LEARNED THAT PLANS CHANGE QUITE FREQUENTLY IN THE military. First, we packed for our flight to Kandahar at 0400. However, after a few hours at the airport, we were informed that all flights were canceled. We ended up having a day to ourselves while we waited for our flights, so today, I planned to go to church, work out, and enjoy a few meals. If we had a cafeteria like this at Fort Bragg, I would have been overweight. To receive a meal, we just had to swipe our ID, and there was no fee. Also, there were a variety of desserts: candy bars, ice cream, chocolate, cheesecake, and pies to name a few. It was even open 24/7, which was convenient for those late-night munchies. With all the food offered, it was helpful to have a place to work out. The base also had a twenty-four-hour gym with weights, cardio machines, and fitness classes. I missed running outside, but since I am somewhat clumsy, I would likely slip on the ice.

MARCH 1, 2012

KANDAHAR

After waiting seven hours for our flight out of Kyrgyzstan, we finally boarded the airplane and arrived in Kandahar. We were driven to our tents, and since it was 0200 hours, we were unable to receive sheets or a pillow. Another dilemma was having to find an empty bed in the dark while other females were sleeping. We were issued a flashlight, but I knew it was buried in my rucksack. I ended up finding a bed and sleeping for a few hours with only a small blanket from the plane. Since joining the military, I had developed the ability to fall asleep anywhere.

This morning, we had IED training. After our training, we went to the boardwalk to have lunch. On the boardwalk, they had little shops filled with jewelry, clothes, and electronics. Also, they had cafes and restaurants that offered pizza, sandwiches, coffee, and smoothies. Believe it or not, they even had a KFC™ and a TGIF™ restaurant. Since the cafeteria was not open twenty-four hours a day, they were our only choices. Near our tent, we had a twenty-four-hour gym, a basketball court, a phone/computer center, and a game room. Each night the lights were turned off at 2200 hours in the tent, but around 0300 hours, I began to hear sirens.

"What exactly is going on?" I asked a female in the bunk next to mine.

"Oh, we are being attacked by rockets," she stated in a calm tone.

I was terrified, but I also got a sense from others who had been here for a few days that it was somewhat normal. During that moment, it hit me that I had traveled to a warzone, and it was now life or death.

The next morning, we went to the range to fire our weapons. We had to zero them, which meant we had to put five rounds in the middle of a target. After we were finished with the range, we were issued thirty rounds that we had to carry in our M-4 rifle. I am horrified that I have the ability to injure another individual. When I was a civilian, I could barely kill a spider. Now, I am aware I may have to kill a person, and that truly scared me.

MARCH 2, 2012

SARKARI KAREZ

Army Logic

Bus Pickup for Flight: 0530 hours

Arrived at Airfield: 0600 hours

Realized that there is no indoor seating available and stand out in the cold for four hours.

Flight: 1000 hours

THE FLIGHT TO SARKARI KAREZ WAS TWENTY MINUTES, AND IT happened to be my first helicopter ride. We flew right over the mountains, which were beautiful. It seemed crazy to me that such a beautiful place could be filled with so much hate and violence. Once we arrived, my sergeant showed us around the base. It was small, and you could probably walk around the perimeter in fifteen minutes. There was a chapel, twenty-four-hour cafeteria, gym, PX, coffeehouse, and post office.

We picked up our bags and moved into our living quarters, which was a containerized housing unit referred to as a CHU. They are basically shipping containers that have been modified with a window and a door. I would be rooming with the only other female foodservice specialist in my platoon. Right across from our room were the bathroom, showers, and laundry room. It was nice that everything was within walking distance since the only light at night was from the moon and stars. I finished unpacking and put pictures of loved ones on my wall to make it feel more like home.

MARCH 3, 2012

PERKS

M Y JOB WAS A FOODSERVICE SPECIALIST OR, IN OTHER WORDS, A cook. After arriving at the base, I was not involved in cooking or anything food-related. So, I worked at our headquarter office and was a member of the Company Intelligence Support Team (COIST). I was "voluntold" (the opposite of volunteering) and had to learn an entirely new set of skills to perform this job. My day-to-day life consisted of being on the computer in the office. It would start to get busier in a few days once the other company we were relieving went back to the states. I worked with the other members of COIST to brief soldiers who were going out on missions. The purpose of the briefings was to inform soldiers of any people or objects that may be dangerous on their convoy. (*Author Note: I really can't say more than that since it is still classified information.*)

The male-to-female ratio for the 4th Brigade deployed at Sarkari Karez was 569 males to 13 females. As females, my roommate and I are required to be together as battle buddies whenever we walked around the base. I also feel safer because we always carried a loaded weapon.

My roommate was working in what is called the Class 1 Yard. Imagine an outdoor grocery store that is stocked with food and beverages that are periodically shipped out to remote bases. Every couple of days, she would bring back cases of water, pop, juice, and snacks. Our room was starting to look like a supermarket. A benefit of this base was what we called the free donation room. It was filled with hygiene products, snacks, writing materials, books, and clothes donated by stateside companies and families. There was an entire bin of greeting cards, so I stocked up. Mailing letters or packages from Sarkari Karez was free, so I plan on writing as many letters as I can. Emails and cell phone technology are the source for the majority of our communications, but it is always a nice feeling to receive a handwritten letter.

MARCH 11, 2012

BLACKOUT

I HAVE GOTTEN USED TO THE DAILY ROUTINE AFTER WORKING IN THE office for a few weeks. Learning how to operate the radio and other programs helped me feel more confident. My unit officially took over after the previous unit returned to the states, and it became busier in the office once we began overseeing the mission.

Each day I learned new things and soon realized that blackouts occurred quite frequently on our base. A blackout occurs when a soldier dies in the line of duty, and the internet and phones are disconnected until their family is contacted. We had been in one for the past two days, and it was frustrating not to be able to communicate with my family. I reminded myself that a family was suffering from a catastrophic loss, and I feel blessed that it was not my family.

My commander asked if I wanted to go out on a convoy to experience life outside the base. I was not thrilled with the idea and just kept thinking of the IED training we had received. Life is about facing your fears, and I had faced many since joining the Army. For example: climbing the tread wall tower, proving that a female can do almost anything a male can do (except I can't just pee anywhere), and the fear of the unknown. Each day I had no idea what to expect, and six months ago, I never would have imagined being in Afghanistan. I would have probably started laughing if you told me I would be a specialist in the 82nd Airborne Division.

MARCH 12, 2012

READ ALL ABOUT IT

AMERICAN SOLDIER SHOOTS SIXTEEN DEAD IN THE RAMPAGE.

TALIBAN VOW REVENGE FOR AFGHANS KILLED BY AMERICAN.

WOMEN AND CHILDREN AMONG SIXTEEN DEAD KILLED BY
U.S. SOLDIER.

THAT WAS ALL PEOPLE CAN TALK ABOUT ON BASE TODAY. THE HORRIBLE part was that the civilians were innocent people that were not considered a threat. First, some U.S. soldiers burned the Koran, and now a U.S Army staff sergeant killed sixteen civilians. One person can really change the way Afghans view Americans and, more importantly, all soldiers.

MARCH 13, 2012

PATCH CEREMONY

TODAY, I EXPERIENCED MY FIRST DUST STORM SINCE ARRIVING HERE, and it was nearly impossible to see down the end of the road. With low visibility, it became difficult to check on the activity on the satellite cameras.

Due to the weather, we decided to have a patch ceremony since many soldiers were on base for the day. I felt very proud to be acknowledged by our commander for my hard work thus far. Still, I found it funny that I wore an 82nd Airborne deployment patch but wasn't airborne. There were a few of us who were not airborne, and others liked to make fun of us by calling us "legs." It honestly never bothered me since I had heard many people talk of their injuries from jumping out of airplanes and felt safer on the ground. I assumed they would either make me go to airborne school or move me to a non-airborne unit once we got back to Fort Bragg.

I had thought about applying for Officer Candidate School (OCS). I am such a planner, but for now, I am just going to live in the present. Whatever happens, I believe it happens for a reason, even if I don't understand what the reason is.

MARCH 15, 2012

MARCH MADNESS

THE LITTLE THINGS MEAN A LOT:

- Receiving a care package
- Receiving a Valentine's Day letter in the middle of March
- Not having to run to the bathroom now that there is warmer weather

I never realized how many things I took for granted until I joined the Army. The little things are what kept me going and enabled me to get through another day. As part of COIST, we had a short amount of time to prepare a PowerPoint presentation for the major. I had one of those moments when I just needed to hear my mom's voice. I tried my best to hold back my tears in front of the major and kept saying to myself, *There's no crying in the Army.* That saying from *A League of Their Own* may just apply to baseball, but I was going with it. As a woman, I was already seen as being too sensitive, and I didn't want to give them any more reason to think that. The presentation went much better than expected, and I breathed a sigh of relief.

I finally got my picks in for the NCAA basketball tournaments after attempting for two days to load the page. The internet was slow, but I was thankful it was at least available. I knew more about sports and world events than ever because of the limited number of channels shown in the cafeteria. I am not afraid to admit that I miss my drama and reality television shows. I will have a lot to catch up on once I returned to the states.

MARCH 19, 2012

ONLY THE BEGINNING

St. Patrick's Day was a few days ago, and I missed my mother's Irish soda bread. The good thing was no one was able to be pinched since there were hints of green in our uniform. We are in the process of moving some of our units to Kandahar, so we have some free time. I decided to take two online classes, which will help if I decided to become a sergeant. I signed up to take a German and Spanish class. I figured since I am German, I should probably learn to speak a few words of it.

I also have a new task of receiving and passing out mail for the troop. Twice a week, we wait for a helicopter to arrive, and then we sort through the mail. I enjoy being on mail duty since a simple letter can bring a smile to a soldier's face.

The weather has felt like summer the past few days, and the wind is really picking up. I am starting to understand why my sergeants strongly advised against wearing contacts. The wind picks up the sand, and at the end of the day, you have sand in places you never expected.

MARCH 27, 2012

YOU'VE GOT MAIL

RECEIVED TWO CARE PACKAGES FROM MY MOTHER WITH BLANKETS, snacks, and lots of candy. It feels wonderful to sleep without a sleeping bag, and the candy is a plus. Many soldiers are addicted to sugar from energy drinks or candy since alcoholic beverages are not allowed. Anyone thinking about going to rehab should probably just join the army. In training and deployment to a Muslim country, alcohol and drugs are not allowed.

We had a couple of missions, but there was no action, which is a relief. We have a three-day convoy coming up to help resupply nearby bases, but with rain expected later today, it may be postponed. It is the first rain that I have experienced downrange, and I realized how much I had missed it. The weather here is very unpredictable. I frequently hear, "You are from Chicago, so why are you cold?" I mention that if it's cold, I stay inside, and if I must go outside, I don't stand around in summer PT attire.

I have been thinking more about OCS and plan to apply once we return from deployment. I am interested in the medical field, which would help with pursuing a career as a dietitian. If that doesn't work out, I may pursue a master's degree in nutrition. That is my plan for now.

APRIL 1, 2012

APRIL SHOWERS BRING MAY FLOWERS EXCEPT IN AFGHANISTAN

TODAY MY SERGEANT SAID IT WAS UNFORTUNATE THAT I WOULDN'T have any exciting deployment stories to tell others. But, to be perfectly honest, I am fine with being bored for the next six months. I am looking forward to saying I went to Afghanistan and worked in an office to help our troops complete their mission.

Sunday is typically considered a day of rest. However, here in Afghanistan, there are no late calls or days off. Same shit, different day sums up my time here. Sunday feels slightly different because of the church service and mail drop. It is refreshing to get away from the office, even for a short time. Working twelve hours a day, every day, I need God in my life to help me through these next few months.

I was pleasantly surprised to receive a few letters from my Grandmother. It is crazy to me how it can take twenty-four days for letters to arrive. I truly enjoy writing letters, and since it isn't used much, it is always nice to receive one. Can you believe it's April already? Time has flown by, and hopefully, it will continue to do so.

APRIL 7, 2012

AN EASTER TO REMEMBER

L AST NIGHT WAS A FULL MOON, WHICH HELPED WHEN I WALKED BACK to my CHU. I attended a Holy Thursday Mass, and the priest mentioned a connection between the moon and Easter. The first full moon of spring is usually designated as the Paschal Full Moon. Traditionally, Easter is observed on the Sunday after the Paschal Full Moon. If the Paschal Moon occurs on a Sunday, Easter is the following Sunday. Easter can fall as early as March 22nd and as late as April 25th.

It has been a few days with about two hours of sleep a night. I am surprised that I have yet to touch an energy drink or coffee. Chewing gum and just staying busy helped me when assigned a night shift. There are three four hour shifts: 2000–0000, 0000–0400, and 0400–0800. I had the 0000–0400 shift, and then it was back to work at 0800.

We had a memorial service for a soldier who was killed in the line of duty. He was nineteen, married with a baby on the way. He was just in the wrong place at the wrong time, and sometimes I wonder why it was him. Why did a soldier who just got to the unit have his life cut short and miss out on fatherhood? Life doesn't always make sense, but I guess God had another plan for him. It was a very sad memorial, and his platoon leader could barely get out the eulogy. As I looked around, I could see most people had tears in their eyes. In groups of three, we walked up to the front of the memorial where his helmet and weapon were placed. There was a picture of him, and for some reason, it was difficult for me to look at it.

April 7, 2012

Attending the service made it so much more real. It made me really appreciate life and all that I have here. I have a job, clothes on my back, food (not the greatest, but still food), and friends and family who love and support me. I complain about the weather here, lack of sleep, and missing home, but the ceremony made me realize how blessed I am.

APRIL 14, 2012

RUN THERESA RUN

WE HAD A FEW MORE SOLDIERS RETURN TO OUR BASE, AND I WAS NO longer needed as a member of COIST. So, my official title would be an administrative representative for our company. I worked on processing paperwork dealing with promotions, awards, and tracking all personnel. It also left me with more free time to work on my foreign language classes. I ran a five-kilometer race with my battle buddy. We were the only two females racing with thirty males. We ran a few laps around the base, and they awarded the top three finishers with medals. The unit replacing us was beginning to arrive, which meant our time here was coming to an end.

My boyfriend and I had been skyping these past few months, but it has been difficult since we were both deployed. It was comforting to be able to talk with someone who understood the slow internet and unpredictable hours. He told me he was falling for me big time and said the three words that no guy ever told me. "I love you" felt so good to hear, but it didn't feel as sincere on Facebook Messenger as it would have in person.

APRIL 18, 2012

DECISIONS, DECISIONS

W E WENT TO THE RANGE TODAY, AND I SHOT THE 240B MACHINE gun from the gunner position in the truck. I hoped it would be the only time I fired a weapon in Afghanistan. I also had to zero my M-4, which meant hitting the target three times in the same area. It was nice to get out of the office for the day and be away from the computer. We were told that personnel in the unit who are not airborne-qualified had to go to airborne school or get assigned to a non-airborne unit once we returned to the states. I am not airborne, and the thought of jumping out of an airplane doesn't interest me. I am also terrified of heights. So, here is my dilemma:

Attend Airborne School:

- Jump out of planes (something I don't want to do).
- Stay with my unit following Airborne School.

Do Not Attend Airborne School:

- Get assigned to a different unit.
- The unit could be in the process of deploying or already deployed.
- Leave my friends that I had made.

APRIL 24, 2012

SAVED BY THE PRIVATE

I HAVE MADE MY MIND UP ABOUT AIRBORNE SCHOOL, AND I DECIDED against it. I felt pressured into going because everyone was telling me I should. In the end, I knew it was not for me. It is my life, and in twenty years, I don't think I will regret not going. Also, my knees and back wouldn't be at risk for injury due to jumping. I knew I took the risk of leaving my unit and not being able to work with friends I had made. But, I was ready to make new friends and experience leadership with a different unit. I really just prayed they were not deploying right away.

Since I was facing so many changes out of my control, I thought I would make my own decision on my own terms. I felt it was time to enroll in a master's program at Trident University International. It was a military-friendly online school that provided soldiers with tuition assistance. I applied for the Health Education program and looked forward to starting classes.

One of my sergeants was moved to oversee us while my First Sergeant was away for a few days. He saw how hard we worked in the office, and he felt like we deserved a day off. When I was told I would be getting a day off, my smile beamed from ear to ear. I had so many things I wanted to do, but at the same time, I just wanted to do nothing. Then, my commander decided to rain on my parade. As I had mentioned before, he wanted me to go out on a mission specifically for the experience. Unfortunately, it turned out to be scheduled on my day off, and I was instructed to go on the convoy. I hoped they were joking, but my commander doesn't joke—ever! Luckily, another private had to retrieve and record serial numbers from some equipment, so he took my place.

My day off was even better than I had expected. It was wonderful to sleep in, be out of uniform, and not be bothered by anyone. I even had enough free time to watch a movie. Ferris Bueller had a more exciting day than I did, but I would not give back those twelve hours of sleep for the world. I never thought I would be so happy about something I easily could have as a civilian. Being a soldier has taught me not to take things for granted, such as having toilet paper and cell phones during basic, hot showers during AIT, and days off during deployment.

I received my birthday care packages early and felt like a fat kid in a pie-eating contest. I received my favorite carrot cake cookies and cinnamon bread. It was a birthday to remember. Last year I had a rum runner drink in Myrtle Beach with my sister, brother-in-law, and cousin. This year I am in Sarkari Karez, Afghanistan. What I would give for an alcoholic drink. The closest thing I had to alcohol was mouthwash. There is also non-alcoholic beer, but I was not that desperate.

MAY 3, 2012

LEG FOR LIFE

TODAY WAS A GREAT DAY THAT ENDED ON A SOUR NOTE. THERE WAS A mail delivery which made me so happy. I loved seeing the mail packages written with "I love and miss you, Mommy and Daddy" and the letters with kisses and quotes from the other side of the world. As soon as we arrived at Sarkari Karez, I entered every soldier's name from our unit to the website www.operationgraditude.com, which donates packages to deployed soldiers. We received about half of the packages, and mine arrived as well. There were letters from children, treats, magazines, DVDs, and a Chicago half-marathon shirt. I laughed as soon as I saw the shirt since I ran the half-marathon last year in Chicago.

It had been a busy day in the office, completing award and promotions paperwork for the month. My first sergeant announced there would be a formation at 1600 hours. As soon as I stepped outside, I was instructed to stand with eight other soldiers. I saw the sergeant major walk towards us, and I realized something big was going to happen. We were all surprised to learn we would be receiving medals for our hard work. At that moment, I felt that I didn't deserve the award. I knew I had worked hard in the office, but I immediately thought of other more deserving soldiers. It didn't feel that I had been in real danger or risked my life for another soldier. However, I was glad my hard work was noticed, but I still felt unworthy of such an achievement.

Another thing I have learned from the military is things can change quickly. After the ceremony, we received an email that the 82nd Airborne Division would be deploying again in October 2013. I was even more certain of my decision to remain a "leg" and decline airborne school. I will be assigned to another unit, which may also deploy, but if I stayed, here I would for sure be deploying again. Deploying once to Afghanistan has been enough for me.

MAY 11, 2012

525,600 MINUTES (BETWEEN BIRTHDAYS)

HAPPY BIRTHDAY TO ME! THE BIG 23! I WOULD NEVER HAVE THOUGHT that I would be celebrating it in Afghanistan. Two years ago, I was having my first margarita in Toronto, and last year I was enjoying the sun in Myrtle Beach. This year it was just another day in the office in Afghanistan. I was tempted to drink the non-alcoholic beer, but even alcoholic beer was not appealing to me. My birthday landed on surf-and-turf night at the chow hall, so I enjoyed lobster tail for dinner with ice cream.

I had time to reflect on this past year and everything I had accomplished. Within three hundred-sixty-five days, I had lived in Normal, Illinois; Wheaton, Illinois; Fort Sill, Oklahoma; Fort Lee, Virginia; Fort Bragg, North Carolina; and Sarkari Karez, Afghanistan. I realized that change in the Army was inevitable. Even the date that we are supposed to return home was tentative.

I had a lot of time to think about what I wanted out of my life. An Army career was not for me, and I planned to be discharged when my contract ended. I want to finish my master's degree. I want to become a dietitian. I want to run a full marathon. I want to travel the world—outside of Afghanistan. I want to get married. I want to be a mother. I want to open a bakery. I want to be happy. I want to live a life that I can look back on and have no regrets. Online, I once read and strongly believed:

> *Dream what you want to dream, go where you want to go, be what you want to be. Because you have only one life and one chance to do all the things you want to do."*

—*ANONYMOUS*

MAY 22, 2102

SLEEP IS OVERRATED

I T IS HARD TO BELIEVE THAT THREE MONTHS AGO, I ARRIVED IN Afghanistan. It has been quite a journey so far, and I hoped that our tour would not be extended. Time has flown by since I started my master's degree. I am enrolled in my first course, *Health, Through the Lifespan*. It has been a helpful distraction from the stresses of deployment.

I finished duty from 0400–0800 hours, which consisted of monitoring the radios. I have a long day ahead of me since I will stay at work until 2000 hours. According to the regulations, we are supposed to get eight hours of sleep per night during deployment. Remember, the keywords are "supposed to." The only night I got eight hours of sleep was on the one day I had off. My sergeant returned and believed I was essential personnel, which meant no more days off while we were deployed.

MAY 24, 2012

IT'S GOING TO BE A GOOD DAY

I TRY TO MAKE THE BEST OF ANY SITUATION. LIVING IN AFGHANISTAN was not my choice, but I did volunteer to be a soldier. My parents, friends, and family members didn't force me to go to the recruiter. I went on my own free will and signed my life away for the next three years. I don't regret joining the U.S. Army due to meeting some great friends and having a boyfriend that has been there for me. I have learned to take nothing for granted. I cherish every phone call, email, package, and letter I receive. I realize how much I am loved even when I am halfway across the world. I have my share of bad days, but there have been some good days as well. For instance, when my battle buddy and I bought a mango smoothie (which was great) instead of our usual slushie, receiving a letter from a friend in Spain that took six weeks, stir-fry Thursdays at the chow hall. I guess everyone needs to have a bad day occasionally; otherwise, we wouldn't know what a good day felt like.

MAY 25, 2012

THE MALE

A GROUP OF SOLDIERS ARRIVED TO REVIEW AND INVENTORY equipment. There was a barbecue for our troop, which I was unable to attend because of my work schedule. I returned to my room and got ready for bed. My roommate came in from the barbecue with our female neighbors a few minutes later. We chatted while the door was open since it was a cool summer night. A male soldier walked by then stood in the doorway and joined our conversion. I didn't know who he was, but I assumed one of the other females knew him from the barbecue. He stepped into our room and shut the door behind him. After we all talked for a few minutes, he left. My roommate and the other two girls went outside to smoke, and I decided to go to sleep. I heard my roommate enter the room about twenty minutes later, and she went to bed as well.

MAY 26, 2012

ATTACKED!

"**H**AVE SEX WITH ME," HE WHISPERED IN MY EAR. I FELT A BODY LAY next to me, caressing my thigh and butt. My body froze, and a million things raced through my mind. My first thought was *I am about to be raped in fucking Afghanistan.* I knew it was the soldier from earlier, and I didn't even know his name. He was strong. I knew that much. If he wanted to rape me, he could have since I was paralyzed. I wanted so badly to move, scream, or do anything, but my body was in a state of shock.

My roommate was asleep in her bed, but I knew she wouldn't wake up because of the sleeping pills she was prescribed. My loaded weapon was next to my bed. He could shoot me right in my bed, and I could be killed by a fellow service member who shouldn't be my enemy.

"No," I said as my voice was shaking.

"Come on, have sex with me," he persisted.

"No," I pleaded.

He left my side and went to my roommate's computer that was next to her bed. The time was 0105, and I just stared at the door, praying he would leave. About an hour later, he shut my roommate's computer and left. I didn't sleep the rest of the night, trying to process the assault. I heard my alarm go off at 0600 hours and headed to the gym as if nothing had happened. I knew I didn't feel like myself, but I tried to block out what happened the night before. After my morning shower routine, I walked to the office at 0750 hours, just like every other day.

At work, I kept replaying in my mind the events of the night before. It didn't help to have a psychology degree and know I was clearly experiencing the classic symptoms of PTSD. I worked with another female soldier in the office and asked her to step outside to talk. I told her about what happened the night before and asked her if it was normal behavior. Her first response was that it was not normal, and I needed to report it. A male soldier who was a paralegal for our division heard the story and had the same reaction. I knew I couldn't go straight to my first sergeant, so I followed the rules and went through my chain of command.

I first ran into my staff sergeant and told him I had something to discuss with him, but I had to inform my sergeant first. After lunch, I told my sergeant, and he reacted as if I was his own daughter describing an assault. He knew the male soldier who had assaulted me since they were both supply specialists. My sergeant probably would have beaten him up too, but the male who assaulted me was off-site for the day. Once my sergeant had the information, he discussed it with my staff sergeant, who forwarded the information to my first sergeant.

My roommate and our two female neighbors arrived at the office and were clueless as to why they were there. I told them the details of the assault, and no one personally knew the soldier who had assaulted me. My roommate had just met him at the barbecue, and our neighbors had never seen him before. Each of us assumed that someone else knew him; therefore, no one asked him to leave our room. I was relieved that he wasn't friends with any of them. I figured they wouldn't believe my story if their friend was being accused of assaulting someone.

My roommate, our neighbors, and I wrote a sworn statement of the events that occurred. After we turned in our sworn statements, my first sergeant wanted to discuss what I had alleged happened. I thought he would be understanding and apologize for what I had gone through. But, the first thing he noticed about my statement was the time.

"Why was the male in your room with the door closed after 2200?" he asked.

To clarify, we were not supposed to have a male in our room while the door was closed after 2200 hours. We could, however, have a male in the room with the door opened.

"It just happened so quickly. We each thought that someone else knew who he was, so no one asked him to leave. He just joined our conversation, shut the door himself, and then left our room a few minutes later."

My first sergeant did not seem satisfied with my answer, but he had to talk to our commander to figure out the next step. I resumed my daily tasks even though I was not mentally present. I didn't even need to tell anyone what was wrong; they all knew I was acting differently. I tried to distract myself by writing a paper for class, but I ended up staring at the screen for what seemed like hours. Finally, I was put on radio guard that night from 2000–0000. I felt like they put me on duty to watch me or protect me in some way. I didn't feel any safer in the office, but I also didn't want to go to my room where the incident happened. I felt like a zombie in the office.

My first sergeant asked me if I wanted to leave early to talk to a female sergeant in our unit who was a Sexual Harassment Assault Response & Prevention (SHARP) representative. I agreed so that I could get away from them and the constant question of "Are you okay?" I talked to her and told her what had happened and how guilty I felt about the event. She told me that my feelings were normal and to be expected because of what happened.

I walked back to my room, and once I stepped in, the flashbacks started. I normally Skype with my family before I go to sleep. However, I was unsure if I should tell them about the assault. Even if I told them they wouldn't be able to do anything except worry more than they already did. My mother would be the most difficult to tell since she was not in favor of me enlisting in the first place. Still, I didn't want to hide or be ashamed of what happened. It was out of my control, even if I did blame myself.

After thinking about it, I decided to tell them but didn't realize how hard it would be. It was even harder than telling them I wanted to enlist in the Army. How could I even begin? "Oh, hi, Mom and Dad, I was sexually assaulted last night when I was sleeping. The male was a soldier who I didn't know, and now my unit is trying to punish me for it. So, how's your day been?" I was fighting back the tears and trying to be discrete about how much pain I was experiencing. My parents reacted with concern and disbelief that my unit would blame their daughter. I was sure if they could come pick me up, they would be on the next flight. However, they knew I signed a contract and couldn't just leave as I pleased.

The next call to my boyfriend was just as difficult since I was already in tears. He knew something was wrong even before I said a word. He responded differently than my parents.

"What is his name? I am going to kill him. Why would someone do that? What are they going to do to him? You better believe I am going to get ahold of him."

I have no doubts that he would have confronted the male soldier if he was on the same base as I was. I was glad he wasn't because I had no desire to be touched, even by my boyfriend. He would probably hug me and tell me everything would be okay. That is a normal response to hearing such news, but it was the opposite of what I really wanted. I just wanted to be left alone, and my unit wasn't having that.

My only time alone was at night in my bed, where the assault happened. Ironically, the one place where I was alone was the place where I had flashbacks. My roommate could tell how upset I was, and she offered me her sleeping pills so that I could finally get some sleep. I took them so that I could rest my mind from the constant thoughts racing in my head.

MAY 27, 2012

COMMAND QUESTIONS

WENT BACK TO MY NORMAL ROUTINE. MY ALARM WENT OFF AT 0600 hours, and I headed to the gym, feeling groggy from the sleeping medication. I walked to the office at 0750 hours and felt paranoid as I knew that the male who assaulted me was still on the base. He may have known that I had come forward, or maybe he was unaware. That was the first time that I felt better carrying my weapon around. My first sergeant was finally able to get in touch with my commanding officer (CO) on the phone. The other three females who had been questioned were brought to the office where we had to speak with him about the incident. I was the first to talk to him, and I quickly realized that he was not on my side.

"Why did you wait so long to tell anyone what happened?" he demanded.

I was in complete disbelief when he asked me this. The assault happened at 0105 hours, and I told my friend at 0800 hours that morning and my sergeant at 1230 hours. My CO couldn't possibly understand what I was feeling, and I honestly was unsure of what to do. The other females talked to him, and after he heard all their stories, he talked to my first sergeant.

We walked back to our rooms together and discussed how unfairly all of us were being treated. On our way back to the rooms, we ran into a sergeant from our unit, and he informed us that the male soldier was staying in the room just behind mine. I froze in disbelief to know how close he was, and I couldn't do anything about it. One of the females wanted to go straight to his room and beat him up, but we calmed her down.

At that point, I wanted to be anywhere else, but where I was now.

I wanted to go back in time and undo my decision to join the service. I was being completely irrational and knew I was right where I was supposed to be. That night I took another sleeping pill my roommate gave me. If I had access to the bottle, I probably would have taken every pill. I didn't want to kill myself, but I wanted to escape and not be associated with people who questioned my actions following the assault. I found out later that my roommate and a female neighbor sat outside my door like guards. I felt comforted knowing that I had friends there who were willing to protect me and not punish me for speaking up. I believe I will be blessed to call a few of the females my friends for years to come.

MAY 28, 2012

ARTICLE 15 SANCTION

THE NEXT MORNING, I WENT TO THE OFFICE AND WAS TOLD THAT MY commander's recommendations were to give all the females, including me, Article 15s for allowing a male into our rooms. I was in complete disbelief and wanted to scream. An Article 15 is a non-judicial punishment authorized by the commanding officer, which can include a reduction in rank and a fine. After the assault, I didn't have to come forward, but I did so because what the soldier did was wrong, and now I am being punished! What happened at 2200 hours was completely irrelevant to the event at 0105, the time of the assault, but my chain of command couldn't see past that. They wanted the easy way out, and punishing me would not lead to an investigation.

The females involved in the situation and I discussed our commander's recommendation. I felt guilty getting them into trouble by coming forward about the incident. They reassured me and said the only people who should feel any guilt should be my CO and first sergeant. We decided to take the issue to the next level and discuss it with our command sergeant major. I told my first sergeant that we wanted to talk to the command sergeant major, and he wasn't pleased. The command sergeant major had an open-door policy, and we had every right to talk to him. Reluctantly, my first sergeant arranged a meeting with him.

MAY 29, 2012

COMMAND SERGEANT MAJOR

A S WE LEFT THE OFFICE, MY FIRST SERGEANT WAS DISAPPOINTED THAT we were going above him to talk to the command sergeant major. I knew he was wrong, and to get justice, I had to start an investigation. I didn't have to speak up about what happened, and if I kept quiet, no one would have even known. I didn't want the attention or sympathy from other members in my unit. But I realized the right thing to do was to stand up for myself even if my immediate chain of command didn't agree. Unlike my leadership, the command sergeant major was on my side. I sat quietly while the other females pleaded the case on my behalf.

During the days following the assault, I was not mentally there. My mind was racing about the incident, and without those four females, I don't believe the investigation would have occurred. I am so thankful for them and the command sergeant major as well. He was stunned that my leadership would want to punish the other females and me for doing the very thing we had been told to do: report sexual assault because it is not okay. He completely disagreed with my commander and my first sergeant about giving us Article 15s. He then decided to start an investigation about the incident because sexual assaults should not be tolerated in any command.

MAY 30, 2012

CID

I AWOKE THIS MORNING FEELING A SENSE OF RELIEF THAT THE MALE who assaulted me was going to be punished. Then I realized that the male probably knew I spoke up, and I had no idea how he would react. At that moment, I was more afraid of him than of the Taliban terrorists. I thought he might try to kill me since he carried a loaded weapon like the rest of us. As I walked to the office, I was told that my phone interview would occur that afternoon. I was nervous, but ready to share my story. I had the phone interview in the command sergeant major's office. The Criminal Investigation Division (CID) were the investigators. I was asked questions about what exactly happened that night and who else was involved. It was the first time I said the entire events of the night out loud. I was shaking and trying not to break up on the phone. I knew this was the hard part, but it would be worth it when they found him guilty.

After the phone interview, I was instructed to go to the health service building. They had a combat stress team composed of therapists who offered trauma counseling. I had never seen a therapist before, but I felt it couldn't hurt to talk to someone. I talked to a male civilian who was shocked by how badly my unit was treating me. He reassured me that I did the right thing by coming forward, even if my unit didn't agree with me. It helped to talk to him. What I liked the most about the therapy session was being away from the chain of command who tried to punish me. With such a small number of soldiers in Sarkari Karez, I knew word would travel fast. The sexual assault wasn't a secret, and I knew it when I saw the looks of pity from others. I felt suffocated and stressed in the office, and it had nothing to do with being in Afghanistan. The therapist recommended that I come back in a few days later.

JUNE 1, 2012

THE INVESTIGATION

THE CID INVESTIGATOR ARRIVED AT SARKARI KAREZ TO START THE face-to-face interrogation. I was asked questions similar to the ones during the phone interview. It was harder to talk in person, and the fact that I was trembling couldn't be hidden as well. For the last part of the interview, I had to take the investigator to my room where the incident occurred. As we were both in my room, he had me lie on the bed and show him what exactly happened. It was the worst part of the interview because being in my room brought back the flashbacks. That finished the interview, and he told me that an incident like mine should be reported. He had to question the male soldier as well as the other females involved after my interview was complete.

I walked back to the office and resumed my normal duties. Work was slow that day, so I tried to distract myself by writing my online school paper. I could hear a few males talking outside as they walked into the office. My desk was right next to the door, and as I looked over, I saw him walk in the door. It was the first time I had seen the male who assaulted me since the night it occurred. He just gave me this look and headed over to the supply clerk to discuss their inventory. I couldn't breathe and honestly thought I was having a panic attack. I didn't want him to see how much being near him affected me. I stepped outside and sat on the bench to catch my breath and calm myself down. The good news was they took away his weapon once they started the investigation. The bad news was he was going to be on the base until the investigation was over. I knew that being at such a small base, I was bound to run into him at work, the gym, and especially the cafeteria. There was no avoiding him.

I remember learning in psychology class about rape and sexual assault and why attackers chose their victims. It has a lot to do with power. I was a stranger to him and honestly just a piece of ass. Maybe he saw me as weak or a female who wouldn't speak up. He might have assumed that I wanted to have sex too. Little did he know that I would speak up, and though I may be weak physically, I am strong mentally. I reported him because not only was what he did wrong, but because he would likely do it again. Maybe the next girl would say nothing, and the cycle would continue. He may think he is powerful now, but I am sure that will change once he meets the investigator.

JUNE 2, 2012

HALFWAY THERE

WITH NINETY DAYS LEFT, THE COUNTDOWN TO HOME IS HITTING me. I am trying not to get my hopes up because frequent change is the Army's way of doing things. They told us that all personnel should be back at Fort Bragg by September 15th. I was ready to go and relieved that we had a short deployment left. I now understand how there are so many cases of PTSD following deployment. I think everyone here is going a little crazy, and frankly, I haven't even been outside of the base. I just keep thinking about home, family, friends, and how close I am to spending time with my loved ones. One of my favorite care packages came from a person I didn't expect. A friend of my father's sent me ten pounds of jelly beans. It not only made my day but my entire week. The only thing that could have made it better would be alcoholic beverages.

I talked to a civilian who went home for two weeks for rest and recovery after a year of working here. He said he spent $200 in one day on alcohol. Before my deployment, I would have called him an alcoholic or just crazy. But, being here had made me realize how normal that sounds. However, I plan to spend my money on a car, a smartphone, a laptop that doesn't show me the blue screen of death, a spa week, or possibly a tattoo. Although I am not planning on getting the 82nd Airborne symbol or anything Army related. Tattooing "Airborne" on my calf like many soldiers did is not something I have any desire to do. I want something that has and will carry meaning for the rest of my life. I have learned a lot about myself and how I am a lot stronger than I give myself credit for.

JUNE 8, 2012

FINAL COUNTDOWN

FOUND OUT THE FIRST GROUP OF SOLDIERS ARE LEAVING AUGUST 25th, so I should be back at Fort Bragg at the beginning of September. That meant a visit to my home town, Wheaton, in October. I am counting down the days until I am home again. Every day in the office seems like I am replaying the day before. The weather is warming up to the point where it feels like a sauna. After a five-minute walk, the only thing you want to do is pass out for a while.

There is another five-kilometer run on Father's Day, which is early enough where the heat won't be a factor. I have missed running races, and hopefully, there will be many at Fort Bragg this coming year. The internet is finally up and running today, so I had a chance to call my friends and family. It made me happy to hear a familiar voice and forget for a few minutes that I was deployed.

It is Friday night, and without a bar, club, or movie theater, I am off to bed. I feel like I can finally get a good night's sleep, knowing that the man who assaulted me has finally left for Kandahar. The investigation is still going on, but now I feel that I can finally breathe.

JUNE 24, 2012

SUMMERTIME

WITH ONLY TWO MORE PAPERS TO FINISH, I WILL BE DONE WITH MY first class towards my master's degree. I never imagined completing an online course on deployment. Being a mail clerk has also helped pass the time. I received a bunch of care packages and letters from friends and family. A letter really did brighten my day and helped keep me motivated. I had my walls in my room filled with letters and pictures from home. My battle buddies tell me how lucky I am to be so loved.

I also ran another five-kilometer race. I finished fifth out of about thirty people and was the first-place female. It may sound impressive, but I was one of only two females in the race. The good news is we are close to finishing our deployment. We find out the flight manifest next month and should be leaving at the end of August. Once we return to Fort Bragg in September, we will be required to have a month-long reintegration. The thirty-day process includes settling back into the barracks, turning in our weapon and equipment, and taking classes to verify our mental stability. We also were informed that October 5–14 would likely be our block leave, which is basically a vacation. I am not getting my hopes up just yet since one thing I have learned about the Army is that change is inevitable.

JUNE 27, 2012

PANIC ATTACK

I HAVEN'T SEEN THE MAN WHO ASSAULTED ME FOR A FEW WEEKS SINCE he left for Kandahar, but now I see him in my dreams. I had this recurring dream where the incident is similar, except he does rape me. I wake up in a cold sweat and realize that it was just a nightmare. Once in the office, the female supply clerk informed me that some supply clerks from Kandahar would be visiting. I grasped that maybe my dream was a sign, and he was closer than I had anticipated. I stayed in the office and prayed he wouldn't visit the other supply clerks. It was lunchtime, and I didn't have an appetite, but my sergeant insisted I go to eat. As soon as I walked into the cafeteria, I saw his eyes stare at me. I tried to pinch myself and prayed that it was just another dream. I sat down and tried to eat, but I felt like I was having another panic attack. I walked outside and just tried to breathe. Even with the sand in the air, it was better to be outside than be in the same room as him.

JUNE 28, 2012

NEAR THE END

SAME SHIT, DIFFERENT DAY. THAT HAD BEEN THE STORY OF MY LIFE in Afghanistan. The best part was that this phase of my life is almost over. I just hope this will be my only deployment. We had to pack one of our bags that would be sent to Fort Bragg earlier, leaving us with one less bag to carry. The items I planned to ship included extreme cold-weather gear, which I hadn't even touched since we left. They wanted us to be prepared for any weather conditions.

I finished writing my main research paper for my online class, and I only have one more assignment left. It is crazy to me that I completed an online class in the middle of the war. Independence Day is just around the corner, and I ran in my last five-kilometer race here. I was the only female represented and placed seventh out of about thirty-five people. My prize was a chess and checker set. I wish there were fireworks, but that would draw unwanted attention to the base.

JULY 10, 2012

HE'S FOUND GUILTY

I received an email from the CID investigator on my case. I honestly didn't want to open it. It reminded me of the letter one receives from the college of your dreams. You are hoping you got accepted, but you don't want to look just in case you didn't. The decision on my investigation would prove to my unit that I did the right thing by coming forward. If he were found innocent, then my unit wouldn't stop reminding me of what I put them through. The back and forth of innocent or guilty was driving me insane, and so finally, I opened the email.

"Our investigation has been completed, and we have found the male soldier guilty on the charges of sexual assault..."

I had so many emotions running through me. I was convinced that I did the right thing by starting an investigation. These past few months of hell that my unit had put me through led to light at the end of the tunnel. I knew my PTSD symptoms weren't going to go away, but knowing the soldier would be punished was empowering. I was informed that he would be discharged from the Army. At that moment, I felt sorry for his wife and child. It was a sense of false guilt because I knew that he brought this on himself. His actions led to his discharge from the service. Maybe it was better if his wife knew the truth. For the first time in months, I can breathe, knowing that my case was not just swept under the rug.

JULY 14, 2012

SO CLOSE TO HOME

IT IS THE MIDDLE OF JULY, AND BY THIS TIME NEXT MONTH, I WILL BE on my way to Kandahar. I am looking forward to returning to the United States. I can't wait to see my loved ones instead of simply hearing their voices. I can't wait to not have to worry about the time difference. I can't wait to text again. I can't wait to eat a home-cooked meal and not have to use plastic silverware. I can't wait to have a weekend off again or even a day off. I can't wait to drive a car. I can't wait to go to a store and buy my own groceries. I can't wait to cook and bake and know what is in my food. I can't wait to smell clean, fresh air. I can't wait not to have to worry about stepping on an IED or getting shot by the Taliban.

What it comes down to is simple. I just want to live without fear and be with the people I love. These past five months have made me appreciate the people and opportunities I had in my life. I know I am truly blessed to have such wonderful friends and family who will always support and love me.

JULY 29, 2012

BLESSED IN AFGHANISTAN

DURING THE CHURCH SERVICE TODAY, A WOMAN WHO SANG IN THE choir broke down and cried. She told us how she felt so blessed to be where she was today. She used to have to worry about providing food for her family and where they would sleep for the night. Then it hit me. I recently complained because my platoon sergeant was an annoying person. It made me think about how my problem is nothing compared to her situation. Even though I was in Afghanistan, I had a place to stay, free food in the cafeteria, plenty of snacks from care packages, and hot running water. I really had nothing much to complain about. Some days I let the heat get to me or fear of being attacked by the Taliban. I feel lucky and blessed not having to worry about food and shelter as the woman in church expressed. I believe God had a plan for me to be here. I am praying that he lets me eventually return home. It seems ironic, but I should be home in forty days and forty nights.

AUGUST 18, 2012

IT'S TIME TO GO

IT HAS FINALLY HIT ME THAT WE ARE ABOUT TO LEAVE SARKARI KAREZ. In just two weeks, I will be flying to Kandahar, and in three weeks, I will be back in Fort Bragg. I have been living out of my bag now and see bare walls where my letters and pictures used to be. It has been amazing how fast, yet sometimes slow, these past six months have gone by. Do I regret coming here? No! I have learned so much about myself. I have grown up in this place where you have nothing else to do but think. The sand is still in places where the sun doesn't shine, and the highlight of my week still is stir-fry Thursday. There are even a few things I will miss, like the stars and moon that act as outdoor lamps. The sunrises have been beautiful to look at when I have jogged around the base.

AUGUST 26, 2012

TWO MORE WEEKS

WE SHOULD BE LEAVING FOR KANDAHAR ON AUGUST 28TH. I AM not a huge fan of it because of the crowds, but it means one step closer to being home. There were also some unhappy soldiers there since the terrorists blew up the Pizza Hut™. Luckily no one was injured since it had only recently been built. I had been relieved of my twelve-hour-a-day duty in the office. Most of our troops are just waiting to go home. I can sleep, watch movies, and just relax for the next few days. I will probably never complain again about working at Fort Bragg since an eighty-four-hour work week is not likely to be required there. I can't believe I have been deployed since February, and now summer is ending.

If I could have only one wish, it wouldn't be to wear civilian clothes, eat real food, see grass, drink alcohol, or drive a car. It would be just to see my family and friends. The cliche is true; you really don't know how good you have it until it's gone. I tried not to take my family or friends for granted, but just being away and praying they would answer my calls made me realize how good I have it. I have the most wonderful friends a girl could ask for that would do anything for me. I couldn't ask for a more supportive family who even sent me fresh blueberries from Michigan that were still cold when they arrived in Afghanistan. As the actress Bette Davis once said, *"It's true we don't know what we've got until it's gone, but we don't know what we've been missing until it arrives."*

SEPTEMBER 2, 2012

LEAVING KANDAHAR

I FINALLY MADE IT TO KANDAHAR AFTER LIVING AT SARKARI KAREZ for exactly six months. I still can't believe I have been deployed since February 23rd. Yesterday, we arrived and moved into our tents. There isn't much to do here but wait to fly out to Manas and then on to Fort Bragg. There is a nice boardwalk with shops and restaurants. My friend and I shared a Kandahar veggie pizza that was baked on Naan bread. It was the most delicious thing I had eaten in six months. We also had aloe vera beverages flavored with white grapes and honey. They were so refreshing, and I really appreciated them since I started to sweat as soon as I finished showering.

There was a United Service Organization (USO) in Kandahar. It is a non-profit charitable organization that provides resources to soldiers and their families. The USO had computers, televisions, wi-fi, and even a movie theater for soldiers. We spent pretty much the entire day watching movies and sleeping in the theater. We had two formations a day just to keep us informed about flights. The only thing that helped me get past the heat and the pervasive smell of shit was the fact that I was on my way home. Right now, that is the best news I have heard in months.

SEPTEMBER 15, 2012

AMERICA THE BEAUTIFUL!

IT HAS BEEN A WEEK SINCE MY RETURN FROM AFGHANISTAN. IT HAS been tough to adjust to the reality that I left behind, but it was so nice to be able to talk to friends and family on my cell phone and even text again. Pizza, shopping, and some partying at the barracks made this a great week.

This weekend I planned to visit my extended family in South Carolina. I can't wait to get a smartphone, much-needed manicure and pedicure, and shop for some new clothes. I don't even know what is in style anymore. I guess anything that is not camo or Army-related is in style for me. Simply feeling like a girl again, wearing makeup, jewelry, and having my hair in something besides a bun would be wonderful.

During my deployment, I learned a lot about myself, and I do not regret one second of it. It sucked at times, and being away from family and friends was the most difficult part. I am a lot stronger than I give myself credit for. And ultimately, if I can survive a deployment, then I can do anything I set my mind to.

SEPTEMBER 29, 2012

BOYFRIEND BREAKUP

IT HAS BEEN A FEW WEEKS SINCE I RETURNED TO THE STATES, AND I have seen my boyfriend one time. The most frustrating part was that the dining facility where he worked was right next door to my barracks. He had many excuses for not seeing me, and I was done with being treated that way. I talked with my roommate, who knew me better than anyone, and she hated the way he treated me. I knew I had to do what was best for me, even though it would be tough. I told him we needed to talk, and he said he would be at my barracks tonight. I know I have to break it off, but I don't want to hurt him.

I met him in his car and tried to let him down easily. I discussed how hurt I felt and how I didn't even feel like I was a priority with him. I honestly didn't feel like I had a boyfriend, but more of a friend who would make every excuse not to spend time with me. Then I said, "I think we should break up."

He honestly seemed surprised that I felt that way. I knew I didn't have much experience with relationships, but I felt that the other person in the relationship should want to spend time with you. The worst part is I will have to work with him in the dining facility. Now I understand why they say not to date your coworkers.

OCTOBER 4, 2012

WRONG TEXT

WORKING WITH MY EX-BOYFRIEND IS AWKWARD, AND HE BARELY looks at or speaks two words to me. On Facebook Messenger, I received a message.

> "I just wanted to say hey and to let you know I miss you, and I tried to hold you in and let you go, but I couldn't let you go."

I messaged him back and explained to him why I felt breaking up was the best thing to do. I thought he got the hint, but then he texted my number. At least, what he thought was my number. After deployment, I bought a new phone which had a new number. Since it was around the time we broke up, I didn't give him my new number. Instead of texting me, he ended up texting my mother, who took my old phone number. My mother received a text from him begging me to take him back and saying how he would change. My father ended up seeing the text message and was very confused until my mother explained what was going on. I told my mother it was best not to respond to him since I had already said everything I wanted to say online. Besides, he had the opportunity to talk to me in person since we were working together but chose not to. I plan never to tell him about the mix-up, so it will just be a secret between my mother, me, and my father, who happened to get pulled in as well.

OCTOBER 13, 2012

BARRACKS PARTY

IT HAD BEEN A LONG WEEK OF WORKING IN THE DINING FACILITY, AND a few friends and I had planned to have a relaxing night in the barracks. We had sangria in the room, and the guys brought over beers. My roommate had injured her ankle that week, and she had an Ace bandage wrapped around it. She decided to take the bandage off while we were sitting and drinking.

After a few sangrias, I was buzzed, and my alcohol tolerance was low since returning from deployment. A male soldier came into the room who worked in the same building as me in Afghanistan. I didn't know that much about him, but he seemed like a nice guy. He was drunk as well, and he decided to take my roommate's bandage and run down the hallway to his room in the building next door. I thought it would be a great idea to follow him and get the bandage back for my roommate.

I caught up with him in his room. Once we were both inside, he managed to remove the front door handle on the inside and put it in his dresser drawer.

"I want to leave. Let me out," I pleaded.

"No," he grinned from ear to ear.

He pinned me down on his bed and started biting my neck.

"Stop. Let me go," I shouted.

I tried to push him off, but he was stronger than me. I told myself that I wouldn't let this happen again, but it was happening. I had no control over the situation, but I wasn't going to let him rape me.

After what seemed like forever, I grabbed the door handle from the dresser drawer and ran back to my room. He was still drunk, and it took him longer to chase after me. Once I returned to my room, my roommate and a few friends were still drinking. They looked at me and instantly knew something was wrong. I had hickeys all over my neck, and I told them what happened. My roommate was furious, and a bunch of the guys wanted to kick his ass for what he did to me. One of his close friends went to talk to him to figure out what exactly happened. All my friends told me they would back me up if I decided to report the sexual assault.

After the experience I had with reporting the sexual assault on deployment, I had no desire to go through that again. What was different this time around was the fact that we were both drinking. I knew that consent is consent regardless of an individual's intoxication level, but I didn't think the Army would see it like that. I assumed my unit wouldn't take me seriously and want to sweep my case under the carpet. I also thought that my unit would just label me a slut since this happened three times, even though I only reported one of them. I was thankful to be able to talk about the assaults with my roommate and close friends. They fought for me on deployment and respected my decision to either come forward or remain silent. If I had been treated better when I reported my sexual assault before then, I would not have hesitated to come forward this time.

OCTOBER 15, 2012

ASSAULTED AGAIN

I WENT BACK TO WORK AT THE DINING FACILITY, AND I WISHED I HAD a turtleneck to cover the hickeys on my neck. I tried my best to cover it with foundation, but there is only so much I could do. I went to the company for a briefing before work, and my sergeant noticed right away.

"It looks like you had a fun weekend," he smirked. His words hurt me since he assumed he knew what happened.

"No, it wasn't fun. A guy did this to me even though I told him to stop," I said.

He simply shrugged it off and didn't say another word to me about it after that. I know sexual assaults are not a comfortable topic of conversation, but sometimes it needs to be discussed. By looking at my neck, anyone could assume I was a slut, which is what my sergeant did. He didn't even talk to me to understand what truly happened. We had classes in the service where we were told to come forward and talk about sexual assault. However, I was made to feel they were my fault. It took me a long time to realize that I did absolutely nothing wrong, and I didn't deserve to be treated the way I was.

NOVEMBER 16, 2012

NO NCO SCHOOL

MY FIRST SERGEANT WANTED ME TO BECOME A SERGEANT. I WOULD first have to go to the non-commissioned officer (NCO) training for a few weeks. Following the training, I would answer questions in front of a panel of higher-ranking officers. The officers on the panel would decide if I would pass or fail. I truly had no desire to become an NCO at the time because I was focused on finishing my master's degree. My unit didn't understand why I couldn't balance work, my classes, and attending NCO training.

Following deployment, my goal was to finish my master's degree and return to school as a civilian. I didn't want to be a sergeant or what seemed like a full-time babysitter. I didn't want to get blamed for my soldier's room not being clean or even if they received a DUI. I believed everyone should be responsible for their own actions. I understood that leadership is necessary, especially in the military. However, I worked with some individuals that had the rank of sergeant and believed they knew everything. I felt like my ideas were simply dismissed because I was a specialist, which is one rank lower than a sergeant.

I distinctly remember certain phrases that my leadership said to me. Most of them are funny, especially regarding how I am always cold even though I am from Chicago. A few more were that I couldn't be from Chicago because I was white or that I had to be careful not to get shot when I went home for the holidays.

A first sergeant was not only a leader of the troop but also a role model. My first sergeant didn't understand why I would want to work on my degree instead of becoming a sergeant. With a simple sentence, I instantly lost respect for him: "You are a failure as a soldier for working on your master's degree." He made that statement with a straight face.

I didn't even know how to respond. I wanted so badly to say, "Fuck you," and walk away, but I had to respect him because he was my leader. I tried to channel my anger into finishing my master's degree and returning to civilian life. I knew that I had to believe in myself and disregard my first sergeant's comments. It is my life, and I am going to live it how I want to.

NOVEMBER 26, 2012

HE'S BACK!

ODAY, WE MET IN THE MOTOR POOL FOR FORMATION. IT WAS maintenance day, and we had to inspect our vehicles. As I walked around the motor pool, I saw the male soldier who assaulted me on deployment.

I froze as I looked at him, and all the flashbacks of the sexual assault consumed me. I walked to my sergeant and immediately said that I needed to leave. He wasn't with me on deployment, and he wanted an explanation. Luckily another sergeant knew and let me go work in the dining facility for the day.

As I walked to my car, I felt the need to constantly look over my shoulder. After my shift, I talked to my commander to see if my attacker was really getting kicked out of the Army. He assured me that it was a long process, and in time he would be discharged. Learning how long it may take for him to be discharged, I asked to switch units. The soldier who assaulted me knew where my unit was, what dining facility I worked in, and where my barracks were. I didn't feel safe, and I was not even in Afghanistan anymore. My commander promised he would be kicked out shortly and didn't think I needed to switch units. I believed him, but I still do not know why.

JANUARY 7, 2013

NO TRANSFER FOR ME

RETURNED FROM CHRISTMAS break refreshed and ready to start work again. As I walked to my company, I again saw the guy who assaulted me. You should be able to trust your leadership, but that day I lost it. I wanted so badly to feel safe again, but every time I saw him, my skin crawled. My unit couldn't possibly understand what I felt and why I hated seeing his face. I didn't know if he would hurt me or maybe go further than deployment and rape me. He had a wife and child, and because of me, he was getting kicked out of the service. I don't think anyone would take that lightly.

I returned to my commander's office and asked again to be moved to another unit. He repeated himself, saying that the male would be gone shortly, and I needed to just go to counseling. I agreed with him about the counseling, but I also wanted to move to another unit. My assailant caused me much pain and left scars that people cannot see. He took a piece of me that I can never get back. When I returned from deployment, I didn't even want my boyfriend to touch me. I feel numb most days and paranoid, knowing I can run into him anytime.

FEBRUARY 19, 2013

PROFILE ISSUED

I N THE 82ND AIRBORNE, IF YOU DIDN'T LIKE RUNNING, YOU WOULD learn to like it. Whenever my sergeant didn't have a plan for PT in the morning, we ran. I personally had no issues with running. We started our run on Bragg Boulevard, which was a very common place for troops to run during morning PT. I felt great running, but then on the way back to the unit, suddenly, my knee popped. It was painful, and I tried to push through it, but I had to stop and walk. I felt like a failure, especially since as a female, I was already seen as the weaker gender.

My company knew that something was wrong since I was the one who always suggested a run. I even beat most of the males in the two-mile component of the PT test. After my half-mile walk back to the unit, my sergeant immediately knew that I needed to see a doctor. I went to the clinic, and the doctor issued me a profile. A profile is a document recommending a period of rest from PT or work if you are injured or ill. It is like a doctor's note to show to an employer to be excused from work. The doctor wrote me a two-week profile indicating I was to be dismissed from PT for that long.

MARCH 1, 2013

ADMIN ROLE

A FEW FOODSERVICE SPECIALISTS MOVED TO OTHER UNITS, AND WE were low on personnel in the administration role at the cafeteria. I was offered the opportunity to fill that role. My duty would consist of filing paperwork, delivering money to the bank, and creating a master schedule for personnel. I was grateful since I needed a break from cooking.

When I started to work in the administration office, the soldier who assaulted me at my ex-boyfriend's party was working in that position. He had a few more weeks until he would be moved to a different base.

I tried my best to focus on learning the new tasks and asked the other sergeants in administration for help. Once he left, I felt a sense of relief. He never did apologize for that night or even acknowledge that something happened. He was the one who started my trust issues with men, and the other two assaults only added fuel to the fire.

MARCH 20, 2013

MOVIE DATE

I ENJOYED WORKING IN ADMINISTRATION, AND I INTERACTED WITH MY co-workers more, which made the day go more quickly. I met another male soldier who wanted to hang out after work. I was hesitant since my last experience dating a coworker didn't end well. I was willing to see how it went and was prepared simply to be friends.

Our first date was at the movie theater, where we planned to meet. I was on time, and I waited for about ten minutes and figured he stood me up. However, it turned out that he went to the wrong movie theater. Following the movie, he introduced me to a few of his friends. He seems like a sweet guy, but I know a lot of guys who seem to be, but they just simply wanted to get in my pants. I want to give him a chance to prove me wrong.

APRIL 20, 2013

HELP NEEDED

DURING THE PAST FEW WEEKS, I HAVE STARTED TO DEVELOP FEELINGS for yet another coworker. We have been on a few dates and talked during work as much as we could before we were yelled at by the NCO in charge.

The coworker came over to my barracks room, and soon talking turned into making out. Everything was going well until he suddenly rubbed my leg. At that moment, it was like I was back in Afghanistan, and the soldier who assaulted me was rubbing my leg and whispering in my ear. I tried hard to ignore the flashbacks, but it felt like it was taking over my body. I pushed him away, and he was concerned that he did something wrong. I tried to explain to him that it was me and not him. I knew that was an overused cliché and a line from many chick flicks.

I also knew I had to explain to him why it was me and not him. It was the first time I had repeated the story in a long time, and it still felt raw. He had no words once I finished the story and simply left my barracks room. I realized that the soldier who assaulted me on deployment had truly broken me. I thought I was ready to move on and forget about the assault, but I realized that it is a part of me whether I like it or not. I know I have to take care of myself, and talking to a therapist is something I need to do.

This night has made me realize that I need help. I still blame myself for what happened, which seems crazy. I was asleep in an unlocked room when he came in and violated me. Even when I read that sentence out loud, it is difficult for me to explain why I continue to take the blame. Following the assault, I was constantly told that since he was allowed in my room earlier that night, I permitted him to come over later. However, the facts were that he walked into our room, shut the door, and left without really saying any words to me hours before the assault happened. It took me months to admit to myself that I truly needed help. I told myself that people are going to judge me because I was seeking help.

Especially in the U.S. Army, mental illness is a stigma people are afraid to discuss. I felt that way for months and struggled to cope with my life following the assault. I was tired of the nightmares, flashbacks, and feelings of paranoia while "he" was still at Fort Bragg. I am done being afraid to seek help, and I finally feel a weight lift off my chest.

MAY 2, 2013

FIRST THERAPY

I HAD MY FIRST THERAPY SESSION IN THE AFTERNOON. THE TWO sergeants I worked with in the administration office knew what happened to me during deployment. They completely supported my seeking help and scheduled me to work around my appointments.

I met with a therapist and started to tell her about the three assaults. The assault on deployment was always the most difficult one to talk about. It wasn't necessarily because of the assault, but more because of the way my unit treated me. The therapist I met with felt that I needed to be assigned to a therapist that specialized in sexual assaults. Now my mind was focused on the assaults and what I should have done differently.

What if I went back to my barracks instead of staying the night after the party?

What if I had checked to make sure the door was locked before I went to bed?

What if I had not chased after the male who took my friend's bandage?

I know that I couldn't change the past even if I desperately wanted to. My only hope now was that therapy could give me a way to live my life even while having the memories from my past.

DECEMBER 10, 2013

MAYBE EARLY OUT

I SPENT THE SUMMER FOCUSING ON MYSELF. I WENT TO THERAPY EVERY week and felt that I was truly making progress. I also took my final course for my master's degree in health education. I now feel more comfortable talking about the assaults with my friends and family. I didn't even question that they would judge me because they loved me even with my faults.

Since I have decided not to volunteer for airborne school, I know that I will shortly be assigned to a new unit. Members of my unit still like to make fun of the non-airborne individuals with use of the nicknames "legs," better known as "dirty, stinky legs." My unit decided to move all the non-airborne personal to non-airborne units. Essentially, we were being moved unless we decided to go to airborne school.

Our unit gave us yet another option, which was to sign an early release waiver. My original expiration termination of service (ETS) date was January 15, 2015. I already knew that I wanted to go back to school and pursue a career in dietetics. I signed the waiver without hesitation and started to research universities where I could earn a degree in dietetics.

For the first time in a long time, I can be the one making decisions about my life. It is hard to explain how freeing it feels to have control back. Military life, in many ways, is not the real world. If you have ever been in the military, you understand what I mean. If you have been a civilian your entire life, then you would need to walk in our shoes or, better yet, our combat boots to understand.

FEBRUARY 20, 2014

GOOD NEWS - BAD NEWS

TODAY COULDN'T BE A TRUER WAY TO DESCRIBE WHEN THERE IS GOOD news/bad news to follow. The good news is that I completed my coursework for my master's degree. I never thought that I would have continued my classes after deployment, but I persisted. The bad news is that I received orders to report to the military police (MP) unit at Fort Bragg. I wasn't getting out early even though I signed an early release waiver.

I didn't know what to say, but a part of me wasn't surprised that the waiver was not applicable. I wanted to fight it since I really had nothing to lose. I went to the retention officer assigned to our unit. He was the person to talk to if it had to do with military order issues. He told me that the waiver I signed wasn't valid since the lieutenant colonel didn't sign it. Once I saw the stack of unsigned waivers, I knew I wasn't the only soldier who wouldn't be released early. I asked for a copy of the unsigned waiver for proof. That is one thing I learned in the service is to have a copy of whatever you sign. Better yet is to have multiple copies just in case.

MARCH 1, 2014

OVER EASY EGGS

IT HAD BEEN A ROUGH FEW WEEKS OF TRYING TO GET AN EARLY release on my contract. I had fought with everything I had and still came up short. I was disappointed since I had just been accepted to UNC at Greensboro, Lipscomb University, Olivet Nazarene, and Northern Illinois University for the fall semester. I now knew that I could attend in the spring and was hoping that the university would allow me to push my acceptance a semester. I tried to make the best of my situation, especially since, in less than a year, I would be a civilian. I knew I would have to start cooking again, and my new unit wanted to see how well I could make omelets on the grill. They didn't know that I had spent most of my military career being an administrative clerk and secretary.

As breakfast started, a soldier had the option of having their eggs scrambled, over-hard, over-easy, or an omelet if they wanted. I thought I was doing a pretty great job considering I was rusty at cooking. For the last order of the meal, I was asked to cook the eggs over-easy. My sergeant stood behind me and micromanaged the cooking process, which happened quite a bit in the kitchen. I gave the soldier the over-easy egg and started to clean up the grill. My sergeant asked if I had been serving over-easy eggs that way the entire meal. I admitted I had been, and I learned how wrong I was. What I thought was over-easy was over-hard, and what I thought was over-hard was over-easy. Too bad there wasn't such a thing as the opposite day because I would have nailed it.

APRIL 15, 2014

GRADUATION PAPERWORK

I HAD COMPLETED MY CLASSES FOR MY MASTER'S DEGREE FROM A university that was an online school and held their graduation ceremony each July. My previous unit knew I had completed my degree, and I planned to go to graduation in California.

When I moved units, I immediately informed my sergeant that I wanted to take leave (vacation days) to attend the ceremony. I reminded my sergeant again since it was early enough to submit paperwork in order to be approved to use leave days. He informed me that we had to go talk to the first sergeant to see if it would get approved. I knew I had to do whatever it took to attend my ceremony. I had walked at graduation before, but this degree meant so much more to me. I started it to keep myself occupied while I was deployed. Once I returned to the states, it was a way for me to focus on something else besides my constant flashbacks.

I went to my first sergeant's office, and I was trying not to get my hopes up. We discussed my vacation days to attend my graduation ceremony, but he didn't seem thrilled with the idea. He informed me that we were training during that time, and he wanted me to stay. I was furious inside since he couldn't possibly understand what it was like to earn a college degree. The other issue was that as a foodservice specialist, we didn't participate in many of the training activities because cooking was our priority. I was extremely frustrated leaving his office, knowing he had the ability to reject my paperwork for vacation.

MAY 9, 2014

MORE THERAPY

CONTINUED TO GO TO THERAPY, AND MY NEW UNIT WASN'T THRILLED that I missed work for it. My sergeant had no right to ask me what I attended therapy for. The only thing he needed as proof was an appointment slip, which I had given him for every appointment. He thought it was unfair to the other cooks that they had to work harder when I was at my appointments. I normally offered to make-up for the time I was at my appointments by working later, but I shouldn't have felt the need to do that. I was simply taking care of myself by going to therapy. Apparently, according to my sergeant, working at the cafeteria was more important than attending therapy.

In the Army, they talked a lot about mental illnesses, especially with the high rates of suicides. My sergeant thought I was wrong for seeking help and missing a few hours of work a week. I eventually was so fed up with him that I told him why I needed to be in therapy.

I knew I didn't have to tell him anything about why I was in therapy, but the constant comments were simply too much. After I told him about the entire ordeal regarding the sexual assaults, he never made another remark about my appointments. I hope he learned that a person doesn't need a reason to attend therapy. In the U.S. Army, we are supposed to be tough and bulletproof, so to speak. Going to therapy shouldn't be something to feel embarrassed or ashamed about.

In my new unit, I was told that my job was more important than my well-being. It was frustrating to be made to feel that therapy shouldn't be my priority. It was heartbreaking to know that many other people felt that way and did not seek the help they desperately needed.

JUNE 5, 2014

NO FIELD TRAINING

OUR UNIT WAS STARTING FIELD TRAINING, AND AS A FOODSERVICE specialist, we had to spend a few nights cooking for the troops. However, I had been prescribed sleeping medication, which required that I get at least eight hours of sleep per night. In the field, eight hours of sleep is very unlikely with the training schedule. My sergeant wasn't thrilled that I wouldn't be able to go to the field. Again, he thought that I was just trying to get out of training. If you asked me, that seemed like a lot of work to attend therapy for a year and be prescribed sleeping medication just to get out of the field training. According to my sergeant, that was exactly what he thought I was doing. He knew that my doctor's note was valid, and he couldn't do anything about it.

JULY 26, 2014

MASTER'S GRADUATION

TODAY WAS MY GRADUATION CEREMONY IN CALIFORNIA, AND I WAS relieved that my first sergeant approved my leave. I had started the degree while I was deployed to Afghanistan. I never imagined that I would continue taking classes when I returned to Fort Bragg. However, being able to focus on writing distracted me from the frustration I had with my unit. I walked across the stage in front of my best friend and my uncle, and I was overjoyed with pride.

I remembered when my first sergeant told me that I was a failure as a soldier because I was pursuing my master's degree. But, at that moment, I didn't feel like a failure, not even for a second. I felt that I had accomplished *my* goal and not my first sergeant's. I didn't want to be a sergeant. My goal was to complete my master's degree, be honorably discharged from the Army, and go back to school to pursue a career in dietetics. My first sergeant wanted to make his goals my goals.

I felt proud that I didn't let his words discourage me from continuing my education. In the Army, making your own choice is not easily achieved. However, the day he said those words to me, I told myself that I wouldn't stop working towards my degree until I walked across that stage. And today, I lived up to the promise I made to myself.

AUGUST 15, 2014

FINAL DAYS

IF MY EARLY RELEASE FORM HAD BEEN SIGNED, THEN I WOULD BE A civilian today. I was lucky that Lipscomb University allowed me to begin my studies in the spring. It was hard to focus at work, knowing I would be going back to school soon. It helped that I had started the clearing process, which involves turning in equipment and attending numerous medical appointments.

My unit was also not thrilled that I had to miss more work to attend my appointments. However, they really couldn't do anything about it. I tried my best not to let it bother me since I wouldn't have to deal with them in a few months.

I started to look for apartments in Nashville, and I can't wait to start a new chapter of my life. I am excited to begin in a place where no one knows anything about me.

DECEMBER 10, 2014

U.S. ARMY LAST DAY

TODAY WAS MY LAST DAY IN THE ARMY, AND IT WAS BITTERSWEET, TO say the least. These past few years have made me into a stronger and more determined woman. Tomorrow I will be a civilian, which seems unreal.

The U.S. Army instilled in me a need to clean and to maintain the hospital corners on my bed. It also made me paranoid that if I missed a call from my sergeant that I would get in trouble. The Army gave me trust issues, which I knew I would have to work through. I wanted to believe that there was good in everyone.

During my time in the service, I met many people who had good hearts. They accepted me and loved me as any great friend would. If it weren't for these extraordinary friends, then I wouldn't have been able to get through my struggles with my PTSD. I know it will always be a part of me. There is no magic pill that I can take to make the flashbacks and nightmares go away. I can't change the past, but I can change my future.

I made the decision to leave the military, and I didn't have to make anyone else understand why. I knew why, which was all that mattered. When I look back at my time in the service, both good and bad, I don't regret a second. It has shaped me into the person I am today, and I couldn't be prouder to be me. After all, no one forced me or persuaded me.

I volunteered for this!

THE END

Illinois State University Graduation

Basic Training

Going Away Party with Family

Basic Training Graduation with parents

Basic Training Graduation

AIT Graduating Class

Exploring Kandahar

Exploring Sarkari Karez

Returning home

Trident University International Graduation

Exploring Nashville and looking at apartments

July 4th family vacation at my parent's lake house in Michigan

Graduating Lipscomb University

Bachelorette Party with my best friends

Wedding Day

U.S. ARMY

ABOUT THE AUTHOR

Theresa Benner McCullough

After separating from military service, Theresa moved to Nashville to pursue a dietetics degree at Lipscomb University using the Post-9/11 GI Bill. While there, she was involved in the veteran's organization, REBOOT combat recovery. After sharing her story with them in a judgment-free zone, she quickly realized it also needed to be shared with others in the form of a book. So, she started writing, *I Volunteered for This: A Woman's Perspective of Serving in the U.S. Army.* Following graduation, she began a dietetic internship at the Memphis VA Medical Center, later moving to Ohio with her husband, David.

Made in USA - Kendallville, IN
1199676_9781734811834
11.24.2020 1501